NO RETURN ADDRESS

NO RETURN ADDRESS

PARTITION AND STORIES OF DISPLACEMENT

Compiled by
Manjira Majumdar

Vitasta

Published by
Renu Kaul Verma
Vitasta Publishing Pvt Ltd
2/15, Ansari Road, Daryaganj
New Delhi - 110 002
info@vitastapublishing.com

ISBN: 978-93-90961-31-3
© Manjira Majumdar
First Edition 2023
MRP ₹ 495

All Rights Reserved.
This collection of stories is entirely a work of fiction. Names, characters, events and incidents are entirely imaginary. Reference to real places, actual regions, institutions or community practices has been made in a fictitious manner. Any resemblance to actual persons, living or dead or actual events is purely coincidental.
No part of this publication may be reproduced, stored in a retrieval system, or transmitted in any form, or by any means – electronic, mechanical, photocopying, recording or otherwise – without the prior permission of the publisher.

Edited by Alisha Verma
Typeset & Cover Design by Somesh Kumar Mishra
Printed by Vikas Computer and Printers, New Delhi

To the rootless, displaced and alienated. This is for you.

Contents

Preface	*ix*
Introduction	*xiii*

Section One: Displacement — 1-70

The Woman Who Wanted To Become A Tree — 1
Shoma A Chatterji

Pishi's Room — 12
Monideepa Sahu

No Return Address! — 29
Manjira Majumdar

Alam's Own House — 41
Dibyendu Palit

Section Two: Alienation   **71-114**

Pressure Cooker   72
Anjana Basu

The Hunter   81
Soumitro Das

The Firebird   93
Saikat Majumdar

The Watch Without Hands   103
Shoma A Chatterji

Section Three: Belonging   **115-144**

About Time, Jessica   116
Rimi B Chatterjee

The Shelf Life   134
Aniket Majumdar

Section Four: Revolution   **145-208**

Revolution   146
Soumitro Das

About the Contributors   *209*
Acknowledgments   *213*

PREFACE

A man gets tied up to the ground
He gives the world its saddest sound
Its saddest sound
—El Condor Pasa, a Peruvian folk song

As India reaches its 75th year of Independence, the world is shedding its borders. In changing times like these, it is only a sense of identity, a sense of rootedness, if you will, that has the ability to keep one grounded. Holding on to that identity or trying to understand it and stay rooted must not be seen as a sign of parochialism or bigotry. To not succumb to what is rigidly held as *politically correct* but ponder upon everything holistically should be the general aim of any literature that deals with a topic as sensitive as the one covered in this book.

Bengal as a province was divided several times by its rulers for various reasons—to manage it better, divide its spoils among the conquerors, or to break the spirit of a rebellious and creatively-inclined community. But what does this division mean to a Bengali? How does it impact their identity, culture, lives and future generations? How did they take this partition and the slicing off of their community? Sadly, these are questions that the rulers ignored to think of—the questions that haunt generations of Bengalis, their memories stowed away in trunks, pieces of documents, dying dialects, photographs or the deepest recesses of their mind.

This displacement brought in alienation, sorrow, longing and a sense of loss in its tow. The resultant rootlessness bred strong emotions like hatred and frustration. Therefore, the theme of this collection alternates between longing and belonging—two different sides of the same coin, with the principle difference being—longing has sad connotations whereas belonging more positive ones.

As stated, everything must be considered in its entirety. This collection of 10 short stories and one long fiction explores the different aspects of one's identity. They place the individual's identity in relation to one's family, community, country, social class as well as one's own self.

Hemingway said, 'No subject is terrible if the story is true, if the prose is clean and honest, and if it affirms courage and grace under pressure.' Nine Bengali writers in their ten short stories and one piece of long fiction have tried their best to tell stories that talk about courage and grace under pressure. The art of storytelling—especially the one where we reiterate our identity—must continue.

Manjira Majumdar
August 30, 2022
Kolkata

INTRODUCTION

I have never felt too Bengali—having spent a good portion of my childhood, adolescence and youth outside the state of West Bengal. So displacement as an aftermath of Partition in 1947 was too remote an incident to occupy my mind, even temporarily. This may be because my parents were already on the right side of the border when the event happened. There were no stories of flight, leaving all behind, in despair and agony. My aunts and uncles, though, had been coerced into leaving the family home due to circumstances and I always detected an anti-Muslim strain in their accounts of their erstwhile 'Desh.' Yet, I didn't see a lot of anger among the displaced residents of Bengal, who may or may not have witnessed a brutal carnage as the one in undivided Punjab. However, I was made to feel special about being Bengali even outside Bengal as a *probshi* (Non-resident Bengali). People would instantly recognize something in me, I knew not what, when I announced to them I was Bengali (Ah, so you are a Bengali?). But, the special treatment also made me an outsider, no matter where I was. The only Bengali artist I would appreciate and learn to respect was Satyajit Ray. But then, Ray was cosmopolitan too.

When I first came to Calcutta at the age of 21, I was struck by how shameless the city was about its poverty and squalor. We were in 1979, just two years into the Left Front rules and it was a pandemonium. I recall seeing a limbless torso with a piece of leather strapped across his back slithering his way on the pavement in *Gariahat*, while women dressed in gorgeous silk sarees, daintily stepped over him to do their shopping.

I remember the band of lepers marching down Park Street on Saturday evening, terrifying everybody into a hushed paralysis of fear. I remember a naked beggar woman tied to a lamppost, having rotten vegetables and fruits thrown at her by an excited crowd thronging around and laughing at the whole scenario. Even mundane everyday things could be torture. The minibuses didn't have enough standing room and everybody, each little body squeezed into the sweating, sighing mass of people, had to stand with their heads bowed. The garbage spilled over everywhere and occupied half the road in many areas. Nobody seemed to notice. There were 8-hour power cuts and I remember my father sitting in the verandah, fanning himself with a hand fan, trying desperately to keep the mosquitoes away.

I couldn't understand how life could go on as usual with this ever present chaos. I was traumatized by Calcutta. It was a city without ambitions, with no future, no hope. All I wanted was to find a way to leave it as quickly as I could. I was an outsider here too.

As a student of Literature, and thanks to my friends, I got to gravitate on the outer fringes of Calcutta's artistic and intellectual community. But, I wasn't impressed. I positively hated Tagore, not so much for what he had written—and I hadn't read—but for the socio-political phenomenon he had been turned into. He looked like a cult guru to me, who had followers and not readers. I hated *Rabindra Sangeet,* it sounded like a child crying for its mother. I started reading Bengali, started to recognize the letters and the words, but it was always a painstaking labour. I read Bengali texts sporadically, a Bankim Chandra here and a Manik Bandypadhyay there…a few poets. I wasn't impressed. There was no Joyce, no Kafka, no Faulkner or Hemingway. Maybe, because I was not a *pukka* Bengali, I didn't have a Bengali sensibility. Why, I wondered to myself, didn't one write about garbage, about the power cuts, the callous indifference to human life?

Having finally settled down in Calcutta, for better or for worse, over time, I have come to appreciate some of the features of the Bengali elite, especially their cavalier attitude towards religion. I also grew aware of what had happened in and to Bengal in the 19th century. The names Rammohan Roy, Isvar Chandra Vidyasagar and Ramkrishna Paramhansa, meant something concrete to me. Now I understand why. They were, each in their own way, iconoclasts who radically challenged the faith of the majority.

So alienation—yes, displacement—yes, in a sense of non-belongingness, all these marked my intellectual horizons and I took them for granted. I cherish my uprooted-ness, my effort not to belong anywhere, to keep my critical mind alive at all times.

The stories in this anthology reveal to me a great deal of Bengali life and its politics post partition. The three sections of this book indicate that more than partition *per se*, the effect of it on the post-Tagorean society and a growing sense of loneliness in urban life are well captured in this book.

The search for a home and rootedness takes precedence over other aspirations such as the pursuit of wealth in Shoma Chatterji's *The Girl who wanted to become a Tree*. The desire to find one's roots forms the central theme of the story. It also serves as a tragic reminder of the consequences of displacement on one's self.

Monideepa Sahu's *Pishi's Room* is redolent with memories of a past that is alive only in its withering physical proof—the photographs and the newspaper clippings. Juxtaposing a drastically real, non-aesthetic present with an aristocratic past—both financially and emotionally, Sahu succeeds in depicting a character who lives steadfastly in the past, clinging on to her memories of what was and alienating the present.

Manjira Majumdar's *No Return Address* tackles the question of Partition. The story of flight under critical circumstances, it focuses on life which once uprooted never finds its roots again. The story becomes a metaphor for displacement. But as tragic as the theme might sound, it is sprinkled with humour and humaneness. A tribute to Manto's famous story, *Toba Tek Singh*, it leaves you reflecting on the tragedy of Partition.

Dibyendu Palit's *Alam's Own House* is a confrontation between two histories—the history of independent India and the liberated Bangladesh. The story focuses on the consequences of displacement—what happens to those who had to leave their homes and more so, what happens when they come back to visit? Are the streets, the scent, the people or the paraphernalia the same or do they change too with the change in borders? Placing the individual as a refugee in a city which was once theirs, the story brilliantly portrays the impact of displacement on the emotions and psyche of the ones displaced.

Anjana Basu talks about Arushi's world in *Pressure Cooker*, a world where the silence permeates through the fabric of her entire being and love is uttered only in whispers, almost illegitimately. The story deals with the theme of Alienation. Describing the nitty-gritty of a contemporary nuclear family, the protagonist oscillates between what could or should be, and what actually is, around her. Basu's writing, very subtly, through metaphors and symbolism dissects the alienation of self.

Both Saikat Majumdar's *The Firebird*, and Soumitro Das's *The Hunter* talk about the protector either revealing itself as a predator or turning into one under the pressure of circumstances. They speak of innocence destroyed and the loneliness of a human being left with only one choice—to submit or to die and to fight the enemy till one's own transformation into the other is complete and irrevocable. The distinction between the human and the animal breaking down.

Shoma Chatterji's *The Watch Without Hands,* speaks of an individual cut off from the society. It highlights how alienation wraps one up in an invisible bubble, how it causes irrational fears and anxiety. But a strong self learns to overpower those fears—and yet keeping one stuck in that bubble of one's own that can never be penetrated. Chatterji weaves that bubble with every word she writes—keeping it truly invisible till the reader pulls out of the story and looks at it from a distance.

Rimi B Chatterjee's poignant sweet and sour story, *About Time, Jessica,* is about the 'Anglo-Indians', who brought their own special verve to the Kolkata scene.

Chatterjee, very interestingly, through the protagonist's disapproval of an event gives us insights on the vanishing community and in the second half, reinstates the need of one's own identity. The conflict between the micro and the macro makes it an extremely charming read.

In *The Shelf Life,* Aniket Majumdar remembers the memory of rootedness within the larger rootlessness that history thrust upon hundreds of families. He is no longer a guardian of memories or the link to the future of the family—his own future being emblematic, a steady displacement in geography and a frequent visitor of the country called nostalgia.

The long fiction, *Revolution* by Soumitro Das is both about alienation and displacement of the gradual encroachment by a relentless force that seeks to destroy a person by stripping one of one's identity—every layer of it. This is a story of homelessness, one's own and that of the less fortunate who have lost their homes to poverty and growth. Wealth and status can protect you only thus far and no further. In the end we are alone and left with whatever pitiful defences that are available to defend our position in the world. This story is set in a country with enormous income disparities.

Bengal's unique history—the last 250 years—has been one of fierce ideological conflict, with endemic political violence as its consequence. The stories carried in this book offer a peek into this world of conflict, both patent and latent. It is but a humble contribution to the effort that English continues to be a language that many Bengali writers are at home with.

Soumitro Das
August 30, 2022
Kolkata

SECTION ONE
DISPLACEMENT

The Woman Who Wanted To Become A Tree

Shoma A Chatterji

When Sheema came home from the other home—a mental home perhaps—they felt she was completely cured. But she knew she was not 'cured' from what they felt was her mental illness. She still wanted to spread her arms wide towards the sky and wave them like the branches of a tree. She wanted to be a tree but they felt she had gone crazy.

She still felt she was a beautiful tree, rooted to the earth beneath her feet. No one could uproot her from her roots. But her counsellor at the mental home had taught her to suppress her thoughts within herself. She

The Woman Who Wanted To Become A Tree is taken from Shoma Chatterji's collection of short stories, *Backlash*.

also advised her not to spread her arms the way she did six months back. The counsellor told her to write her thoughts or draw trees whenever she felt like becoming a tree. That would make her look 'sane' and acceptable by her close family. But she was not happy. She just wished she was a tree and there was nothing anyone could do about it. Her husband Subroto, was both concerned and scared for his wife of ten years because he was unsure if the treatment in the home had cured his young and pretty wife of her crazy idea that she was indeed a tree.

Sheema, however, had always been like this. Her parents were worried but they disciplined her in a way that she would feel that she was a girl—a human being and not a tree. They were worried but it did not occur to them that this perhaps needed a cure. She went to school, studied well but could not make any friends because they were a bit scared of her. They felt something was wrong with this beautiful girl who kept standing in the prayer hall after the prayers were over and everyone else had moved away.

It all went back to a short Gujarati play she had watched on Doordarshan as a child. In the play, the head of the family stood outside their small hut one day, spread his arms wide, looked up at the sky and muttered, as if to himself, '*Mu vrksha chhun*' meaning, 'I am a tree.' His wife and three kids pooled their physical strength to shake him and bring him back to his former self. But nothing happened.

They requested the panchayat head to physically come and persuade the man to come to his senses. But he refused to budge—emotionally and physically—from his place. The entire panchayat organized a meeting in the compound to discuss the problem. Nothing changed.

The middle-aged man stood his ground as if frozen in that space and in the posture he had assumed. He stopped talking completely and did not eat. He began to lose weight and one could actually see him slimming down like the trunk of a very thin tree. One of his children would pour water on his feet every morning, clandestinely so that her mother would not come and shoo her off. She would look up to what was once her father's face and imagined that she saw the hint of a smile. But she also knew that this was her imagination playing tricks on her.

The police were summoned and tried to arrest him. But, they could not move him from where he stood. Slowly, birds came and began to perch themselves on his widespread arms. They cried, chirped and sang together, flew away and came back again the next day. His wife and children tried to shoo them away but they behaved as if they neither saw their waving hands nor heard the sounds of their shooing.

His desperate and shocked family was forced to uproot itself from the home that had been theirs for three generations—move on to begin life anew.

Over time, as the birds came and perched themselves on his skeletal arms, his arms began to resemble the branches of a real tree. His clothes were tattered, torn and dirty but within the holes in those tattered rags, one could actually see what appeared to be the inside of a tree trunk. The Family was now quite scared, the small plot of land and the tiny hut was sold at a throwaway price. The man-tree kept standing there, oblivious to the twists and turns of his life or his destiny. As time passed, it was just the tree standing on the compound of a small mud hut that had now been reduced to pieces of wood, clay, mud and twigs. The short telefilm had ended on that note.

Sheema's mother had entered the room and noticed her daughter looking awestruck at the television screen. She switched it off. Sheema was hardly fourteen then, but her mind was made up. She wanted to be a tree.

Her parents, she had heard, were refugees who had come from East Pakistan during the Bangladesh Liberation War in 1970. The crossing was done without any legal documents which made them refugees without any ration card or document that could give them the identity of being Indian citizens. Nor could they go back for they were now without a homeland. She was born ten years later, when her parents had almost given up all hopes of ever having a child. Naturally, they were overjoyed. It often made her wonder why they had named her 'Sheema' which meant both 'limit' and 'border.'

It also intrigued her that they did not have more children. Maybe then, she may not have wanted to become a tree. Her entire childhood had been rootless. Journeying from one place to another because their illegal status made them live a life of fear—the fear of getting caught and being sent away to Bangladesh. But she was born in India so she was an Indian and not a refugee.

But her parents were refugees. They were forced to leave their homeland and make a home for themselves in a strange country. The only thing common between their refugee status in India and their native status in Bhola, a small island, now in Bangladesh was the language—Bangla. That too only if they continued to live in West Bengal which they did. But the Bangla her parents spoke was different from the Bangla she spoke. They spoke with an accent that people took time to understand but she spoke in the Bangla which everyone understood.

Her father got a job as a mathematics teacher in local schools wherever they shifted. It was not very difficult because he was a good teacher and in remote, small towns, teaching jobs were easy to get. But she knew that some of his students laughed behind his back because of his strongly accented Bangla called 'Bangal' here. They moved from a small town in Murshidabad district to the small town of Seoraphuli in Hooghly district to Jadavpur in Kolkata which had a scattered colony filled with refugees from East Pakistan and then Bangladesh.

In Seoraphuli, she learnt to swim in the Hooghly river which was near the place they lived. She was thrilled when she felt the rippling waters on her sari-clad frame—wetting and drenching her. She was petite and pretty but a bit dark skinned and quite attractive if one looked at her closely. But she was least concerned about her looks although she did take care of her hands. She felt that they would one day spread out to become the branches of a tree that she would change to.

'Who is a refugee?'

'A refugee is someone who has been forced to flee his or her country because of persecution, war or violence,' her father had once explained to her. That meant that she was not a refugee. Her parents were but she wasn't. Then why did she need to flee from one place to another, live almost in anonymity lest they were caught and transported for being illegal refugees? But she needed to follow her parents and go with them wherever and whenever they displaced. She had realised that she was as rootless as her parents were—just because she happened to be their child.

When she graduated from high school, Sheema's parents sent her to college in central Kolkata. She would need to stay in a hostel. This was again an uprooting not only from Jadavpur but also an alienation from her parents. She did not like the idea but then, she had no choice, did she?

She again wished that one day she would become a full-fledged tree, with or without flowers and fruits but with birds coming and perching on her branches, building their nests for their little ones and guarding the nests the best they could. At every place she lived, she grew fond of the trees, plants and flowers in and around their home.

But from the minute she heard they had to move on, *once more*, she felt sad. She wished to turn into a tree and stand beside them. She prayed that she would not need to move on. Her smile faded when the rains came and washed over the trees. She saw them shiver in the wetness and the moisture that the rains brought along with them. In winter, she saw the trees shedding their leaves and standing with their leafless branches silently, as if waiting for spring. Spring—when they would sprout new leaves or flowers.

She did not know what pulled her to trees but she always felt it was because they were rooted to wherever they stood. They never needed to move on from place to place, like gypsies though they were not gypsies.

Her sketchbooks had been full of pencil sketches of trees of different kinds. Her drawing teacher had complained that she did not follow the drawing given in the class. But she was good and they could not complain much. Her adoring mother had taken some of these drawings and framed them to hang on the walls of their small refugee home. The word 'refugee' was a noun but it could also be used as an adjective if the way her mother used it was right.

Then she had gotten married to Subroto. She was happy to finally find her roots, once and for all. Subroto, like her, was the only child of his parents and they lived in a sprawling mansion in Bhawanipur in south Kolkata. It was a family mansion built a hundred years ago by Subroto's great grandfather. Sheema was happy to have finally found her roots. As it was a heritage house, they would not have to uproot themselves and move again. She would try her best and give the marriage her all. But for that, she needed to get rid of her lifelong wish of becoming a tree.

'You are an immigrant now,' Subroto had once explained even when she had not asked. He went on to explain that an immigrant is the one who had shifted from one place to make her home in another place permanently. She did not bother about all this because from childhood she was conditioned to believe that her home with her parents was a temporary one and a day would come when she would have to go and live somewhere else, with someone else, forever.

Two days after her return from the home, Sheema found herself relaxing in her bed at the odd hour of eleven in the morning. At normal times, she would have been in the kitchen, supervising the cooking, or switching on the washing machine, or whipping up batter for a lovely cake.

But now, she had all the time in the world to relax, lie down and do nothing but think and watch. She did not like to watch television. They did not show anything on trees.

From the first-floor window of her bedroom, Sheema looked out at the banyan tree spreading its branches to reach the sky, with birds coming and settling on its branches, only to fly away. She tried to look for a nest hidden in the folds of the branches but could not find any. Were those birds immigrants like she was—having come from her Kolkata home to make a new home in Mumbai—thanks to Subroto's transferable job, taking them from Chennai, Bengaluru, Allahabad, Delhi, Kanpur and then back to this nest in Kolkata? She suddenly wished she could have the freedom of those birds flying around the tree, to spread her arms and fly away.

It was a bit problematic when she mulled over what Subroto had said—that she was an immigrant. But after some time, she accepted it as a part of her destiny.

She pulled the curtains of the window close, turned away and went to lie down on her bed for a short afternoon siesta—a luxury for her till a few months ago. The birds perched on the tree outside, looked at the curtains pulled close and flew away, free and liberated, forever.

Her last thoughts before she dozed off were, 'What is my status? Is it bound to be this home and this family? Or, can I go off when and where I would like to?'

She tried to remember the two short sentences she had scribbled on the back of an old boarding pass, the very organized Subroto had forgotten to file.

She forgot to pull the quilt over herself, or maybe she was too sleepy from the tranquilizers she had to take. She curled her feet, drawing them to her tummy.

It was cold and she felt a chill. She did not realize that she was lying in the foetal position, just as she had done in her mother's womb before she was born. Or, how children stay in their mother before seeing light. She tried to look at the tree outside and then remembered that she had pulled the curtains close.

When Subroto came home in the evening and stepped into Sheema's room, he found her curled in bed, fast asleep. He had no wish to disturb her though he realized she may have overslept and needed her dose of medicine. He did not realize that Sheema had passed away gently in her sleep. When he touched her and found her body cold, he got scared and called for her doctor.

As the family physician wrote out the death certificate after three hours, Subroto tried to shift her body with the help of the servants. Under her pillow, he discovered a forgotten boarding pass with just two lines penned in Sheema's beautiful hand on the back.

I am not a refugee.
I am an immigrant.

The next morning, no one noticed that a small sapling had sprouted up in the huge shade of the banyan tree.

Pishi's Room
Monideepa Sahu

I grabbed the handrail for balance in the rattling bus. The cold shower I had taken an hour ago, the scent of soap and lavender cologne, were now sweat-smothered memories. My parents and I were taking this bus halfway to Pishi's place to save on the taxi fare to reach the other end of town. We had spent enough on sweets, a sari for Pishi, and gifts for her grandchildren—my bratty little second cousins, whose names I forget. Pishi was my Ma's aunt, and therefore my grandaunt. But everyone called the old lady Pishi, which meant aunty in Bangla.

Pishi's Room first appeared in *Behind the Shadows: Contemporary Stories from Africa and Asia*.

This is what we do when we visit Kolkata—rush all over the town meeting obscure distant relatives who stare at the wall and mumble, 'My! How she's grown.' Before the air cooler dries the sweat from my forehead, I'm sure they'll forget my existence.

The bus jerked to a stop. My bra constricted my chest making me gasp for breath. Nearby, a portly matron wiped her face with the corner of her sari and roared, 'This heat is killing me.'

'Bolo Hari! Hari bol!' Two young men began reciting the Hindu funeral chant. 'Oof! The coffin is heavy,' one of them said, while his friend grunted and pretended to lift the load. I watched the other passengers' reactions to this display of typical Kolkata humour before allowing the giggles to burst out. The matron looked down, avoiding the grinning faces around her. After all, she wasn't the only one suffering.

The lines on my Baba's face too eased into a smile. My Ma frowned, pursed her lips, and jabbed her elbow into my side. 'Don't laugh, Mithu. Learn to behave in public,' she said, 'You're sixteen, a big girl. A few years from now, we'll have to find a husband for you. Your in-laws won't tolerate such cheek.'

Baba gave me a knowing look as though to say, 'I'm with you.'

I smiled back at him—hidden from Ma, of course! I've learnt to brush aside Ma's eternal scolding. I know how Baba, the ultimate henpecked husband, rolls his eyes behind Ma's back when she plans these whirlwind visits. But the worst is if we don't go with her, we'll face another outburst of Ma's volcanic temper—after all, she is Pishi's dearest niece. At least she used to be, until Pishi turned eighty and began to forget who Baba and Ma were.

The bus rumbled on. I resigned myself to the prospect of a wasted afternoon. At last, we got down at a stop in central Kolkata. The sticky, humid air smelled of spicy onion pakoras sizzling in wayside tea stalls. I felt like stopping for a plateful with an extra helping of the hot and sour mint chutney. But Ma gave her usual glare. I decided to choose my battles carefully and moved on. Next summer, I'm going to insist on joining my friends for a trek in the hills and not allow Ma to bulldoze me into attending another pointless family reunion.

A stream of people swirled around us as I stood with my parents on the roadside waving down passing taxis.

'Going to Baag Bazar?' Baba asked.

'Boshun,' said the turbaned Sikh driver in perfect Bangla, unlocking the rear door for us.

The breeze rushing in through the window cooled my skin. I looked at the bumper-to-bumper traffic and inadvertently, inhaled exhaust and dust. Dark, decrepit buildings dating back to the days of the British Raj loomed over the roadside. A century's accumulation of lichens and grime gave their walls a mottled grey finish.

Everything here seemed to be a decaying relic from the past—like Pishi herself. As we drove by, I caught glimpses of bulging-eyed gargoyles and fluted gables. A blue sari fluttered from a clothesline below a window.

When we're in Kolkata, Baba and I enjoy staying as houseguests with Baba's older brother. My uncle's well laid-out neighbourhood in South Kolkata reminds us of our home in Delhi. My cousin Tukuda is a year older than I am, and we argue on everything from politics to movies and exchange confidences about our current crushes. Tukuda's modern house is the antithesis of Pishi's crumbling home in a run-down neighbourhood. The star attraction is a lake two blocks away. Tukuda and I stroll by its banks in the evenings and watch herons wade among the water lilies, while kingfishers swoop down in flashes of jewel blue.

I'd tried to persuade Tukuda to join us. 'We went to visit Pishi just six months ago,' Tukuda had said. 'Who wants to hear the old lady ramble about the good old days before Partition?' Then he had cut me short and picked up the phone for another marathon call to his girlfriend.

Our taxi stopped before Pishi's home in a building as ramshackle as any in this part of town. Pipal saplings pushed out their heart shaped leaves through the peeling, cracking walls. The place reeked of cockroaches and the fishy-slimy odour of algae in stagnant water tanks.

Tenants here clung to their dilapidated apartments like worms to rotting mangoes. The laws made it difficult for landlords to evict them or raise the ridiculously low rent, so nobody bothered about repairs and maintenance. I shuddered wondering how people survived in places like this with their sanity intact.

I climbed up the staircase gathering my skirt and steering clear of the splotches of orange betel juice on the walls. Eager faces peered out from the door of Pishi's apartment. My aunt stood at the open door, plump and smiling. Her two kids, my pesky little second cousins, hid behind the folds of their mother's sari. Ma and my aunt exchanged hugs. I had to touch the feet of my elders, but where was Pishi?

The little imps, a boy of three and a girl aged seven, tugged at my skirt and ponytail. I tried to hide my annoyance, but kept them at arm's length all the same. The last time I was here two years ago, that girl had smeared chewing gum all over my hair. She held a fistful of crayons and smiled, probably scheming to scrawl on my back. The boy's limpid eyes pleaded for a cuddling, but he didn't fool me. He ought to be toilet trained by now, but I didn't want to risk him wetting me again.

After much cajoling, the children guided us to the room they shared with Pishi. A huge bed took up most of the room. Each of the bed's heavy carved legs was placed upon three bricks stacked flat upon each other to raise the bed by an extra foot or so. My Ma too raised our beds like this to make it easier to clean underneath.

Her white saris hung in neat folds from the clotheshorse, but there was no sign of Pishi herself until the kids crawled under the raised bed and called her.

The kids shouted and tugged at her sari. I made no effort to hide my surprise, as Pishi pushed herself out in a bent, squatting position from under the bed. With arms akimbo, the old lady moved her stiff body like a waddling duck. I choked down the laughter bubbling up inside me and ended up with a red face.

Ma and my aunt chattered on as though they had expected Pishi to come up with this new caprice. Pishi wore her usual straight-laced expression and managed to emit a dignified aura despite her bizarre action.

She looked me over with rheumy eyes, stroked my pink cotton skirt, and said, 'You're sixteen now? Ah, when I was your age, I came to this house as a young bride. I was shorter and plumper than you, but my skin was just as clear and fair. I felt awkward and nervous bundled up in a red silk sari with a golden border, my head covered with my sari pallu to show respect to elders. I never met my husband before we were married. In those days, they usually arranged marriages that way. So he was a stranger to me like everyone else in my new home.'

I looked closely at Pishi. She was bent with age. Folds of crushed paper skin distorted her features. Her scanty white hair was cropped short in the style enforced upon widows of her times. I tried to picture her at sixteen, her skin smooth and brown eyes twinkling with mischief.

My Ma and aunt left the room with the little kids in tow. I was alone with Pishi. Nobody seemed interested in talking to either of us. I could guess exactly what would happen if I followed the others into the sitting room.

Outside, Pishi's son and daughter-in-law, my uncle and aunt, would ask me to sing, because all well-bred Bengali girls are expected to sing. I would smile and feel like saying, 'If everyone sings, who'll listen?' But I would glance at Ma's scowling face and smile in silence. Then, they would talk with my Ma about the old times that Baba and I never shared. Baba was the son-in-law of the family, so they made him sit in the stuffiest sofa, offered a plate piled with sweets he'd rather not have eaten, and then left him alone. That's what had happened the last time I was here, and I expected little to change now.

Meanwhile, Pishi lifted the Sholapuri bedspread hand-woven with brown, red, and golden floral patterns. It was as though she had pulled aside an ornate curtain to reveal a mysterious world. She then eased her bony, arthritic figure under the bed and invited me in with a wave of her hand. It was either this or I had the option of genteelly singing indolent Tagore songs for the gathering in the sitting room. I toyed with the idea of shocking them with a lively popular number from the Hindi movies, but the prospect of Ma going ballistic deterred me.

Pishi's new whim might be crazy, but it was unique. I decided to play along and bent my slim body to slide under her bed. It was easy for me to crawl inside. I lay down on the straw mat she spread for me and leaned on my arm to raise myself. It was cosy inside, and though we couldn't sit up straight, we managed to recline and relax in snug comfort.

It was like another room under the bed. As my eyes adjusted to the shadows, I saw an old-fashioned steel trunk in the corner. A gaudy framed picture, obviously taken from a calendar, hung on the wall below the bed. In the other corner stood a low shelf with jars of pickles and preserves made by Pishi herself.

'They painted the house and ordered for new furniture to welcome me as a young bride.' Pishi's voice quavered and she stared at nothing. I wondered whether this place was ever painted again after Pishi's wedding.

Her bent, knobby fingers twisted a ball of thread the size of an orange. It was Pishi's collection of bits of strings from parcels and packing boxes, and it grew larger every time I visited.

'In those days, my late husband and I had this entire room to ourselves,' Pishi said.

'In a house full of strangers, it was my only refuge. Now, this is my room.' She waved at the underside of the bed. 'I sleep with the children upon the bed at night. But during the day, I need a room of my own under the bed to pray and meditate in peace.'

I nodded, beginning to see sense in her eccentric ways. The bed above us muffled the noise from the rest of the house and the busy street outside. The floor was pleasingly cool, and shadows created the illusion of privacy. If I wanted to read a book or just be left alone in this crowded house, this 'room' would be the best place to choose.

Pishi opened her trunk and took out packets of letters from her two married daughters and her elder son, who was a professor in Bombay. Inside, I could see two carved wooden figurines, a bundle of palm leaf manuscripts, and a set of prayer books. I knew they were relics salvaged from their ancestral home which the family was compelled to leave behind in East Pakistan after the Partition of India. As she passed her wrinkled hands over them, I waited for her to unfold the palm leaf manuscripts and show me the Sanskrit calligraphy done by our scholarly ancestors. I expected her to tell me again how those carvings of an elephant and a prancing horse once graced the sitting room of her old family mansion in what later became East Pakistan.

Pishi's trembling fingers passed over the figurines and the manuscripts to grasp a tattered scrapbook pasted over with yellow newspaper clips. I didn't remember seeing this before and waited with more than polite interest for her to proceed.

'Tell me,' Pishi said, turning the crackling pages. 'There used to be this wicked fellow called Hill Taar, who fought wars against every country. What's he up to these days? I can't read the newspapers any longer, and the TV hurts my eyes. Is he still making trouble?'

I sighed. Pishi was so old, so hopelessly out of date. 'That was Hitler, Pishi,' I told her. 'They defeated him in the big war, and he killed himself ages ago.'

Pishi nodded. She turned the pages to a picture of Indira Gandhi. 'She's a great lady,' she said. 'She's leading our country to prosperity.'

'Pishi, Indira Gandhi was shot by her bodyguards six years before I was born.'

Pishi gasped and wiped a tear from the corner of her eye. Didn't anyone bother to talk to her, to tell her such things before? Or had she forgotten? 'Show me your embroideries and that set of crocheted mats,' I said, choosing a topic within her depth. She opened the trunk and spread out a cross-stitched portrait of the portly, elephant-headed Lord Ganesh.

I ran my fingers over the Lord's round paunch and the neatly embroidered bowl of sweets in his hand. I loved the soft pastel green, the yellow of the robes, and the merry smile on the Lord's pale pink face.

'Tell me Pishi, have you made a new batch of pickles this season? I want some sweet mango preserve if you have any,' Pishi reached for the shelves and took out an old-fashioned brass plate with fluted edges. It was polished to gleam like gold. Pishi filled the plate with dollops of homemade preserves; sweet and hot mango, sour tamarind, and cranberries in sugar syrup. Then, she took two coconut nadus from a glass jar, handed me the plate, and tilted the earthen pot to fill a glass of water. The sweet, round nadu melted in my mouth. Pishi always roasted the grated coconuts just right. It was crisp, but never bitter with over-heating. The water smelled of rain-drenched earth.

'Eat well, child.' Pishi patted my head, running her stiff fingers through the curls in my ponytail.

My aunt entered the bedroom and said, 'What are you two doing here? Come, join us in the sitting room.'

I followed Pishi out from under the bed, and together we went to join the rest of the family. My uncle had come home early from work to meet us. Baba finally found someone to talk to while eating all those sweets. My aunt and Ma sat on either side of Pishi and tried to charm her into parting with her best recipes.

'Please Pishi,' Ma said. 'You've become so forgetful. At least write the recipes down to pass them on to your granddaughters.'

'Leave her,' said my aunt, confident that Pishi couldn't hear her hushed words. 'She's losing her wits with age. We've reasoned with her so much, but she insists on spending most of the day under that bed.'

'Mithu, you've grown so tall,' my uncle said. I stiffened, dreading the inevitable. Baba gave me an encouraging wink from across the room, while Ma glared as if to say, 'Don't you dare refuse to sing.'

'Tell me how you're doing at badminton. Have you made it to the school team?' Uncle asked.

When someone was ready to listen, I could talk forever about my favourite sport and the last season's matches. From the corner of my eye, I saw Pishi rise stiffly from her chair and hobble away. Seeing another chance to be alone with Pishi, I picked up my plate full of rosogollas and followed her to her room. I crawled under the bed to join her and asked, 'Why did you leave, Pishi? Did all that sports talk bore you?'

'No, no. I don't understand sports, but that doesn't matter. I felt happy to see you enjoying yourselves.' Pishi paused and rubbed her withered hands. 'I tire easily these days. I need rest; some peace and quiet.'

She lay down on the straw mat and stared up at the slats lining the bottom of the bed. 'You can look through my newspaper clippings,' she said, handing me her scrapbook. 'I haven't added new cuttings in the last few years, but the old items may still interest you. And if you want more preserves, help yourself.' Pishi coughed and wheezed softly. I stroked her thin chest, her forehead.

Turning the scrapbook's yellowing, brittle pages was like taking a journey into the past. There was a long article with a picture of the Tricolour of independent India replacing the Union Jack above the Parliament House. The assassination of Mahatma Gandhi, the wars with China and Pakistan; Pishi had faithfully recorded history as events unfolded before her.

'Oh Pishi,' I said. 'This scrapbook is a gem. You must be among the most well-read ladies of your generation.'

'My in-laws pulled me out from school after I got married,' she told me in a confiding whisper. 'Books were a waste of time for girls, they said, and told me to concentrate on keeping house and cooking.' Pishi nodded and sighed. I wondered how I would have survived without books and waited for her to continue.

'My husband was just eighteen then, and too much in awe of his parents to stand up for me. He used to pass me the newspapers when nobody was watching, and helped me make this scrapbook. See,' she pointed a gnarled finger at some words written neatly in fading ink. 'That's his writing. He used to bring books from his college library and sneak them to me in the folds of his homespun dhoti. In those days, he and his friends refused to wear western clothes as a mark of protest against India's British rulers. At night, after everyone else was asleep, he would read to me from Bankim Chandra, Sharat Chandra, and Tagore's works.'

Pishi sighed, perhaps in an effort to hold back tears for the bygone days. I placed my arm around her thin shoulders and felt the ebbing warmth of her body. She put her hand upon mine and said, 'He had a deep, rich voice, my husband. My reading, this scrapbook; these were secrets I shared only with him. Nobody else knew except my sister, who died three years ago. And now, I'm telling you.'

I looked up at Pishi's late husband's blotched, sepia-tinted photograph on the mantelpiece and wondered about his times. He died when I was four years old, and I didn't remember anything about him. Pishi grew up in another world; a world I had only read and heard stories about. Yet like me, she wasn't always the girl her elders wanted her to be.

'Relax Pishi,' I said. 'You don't have to worry about me. I just want to be near you, listen to you.' I stroked her hand and ran my fingers through the white wisps of hair. Oblique rays of sunlight entered under the bed, lending translucence to her skin. She looked so fragile, as if she would melt away into the shadows.

'What can I say that will interest a modern girl like you? In our times,' she said after a pause, 'girls were packed off to their husbands' homes as soon as possible. We didn't get a chance to study much. Embroidery, cooking, and the three R's, that's all I know.'

I knew such a fate wouldn't be thrust upon me, but in her times Pishi had fewer choices. 'You know so much,' I told her, 'Your pickles and preserves are the best.

Even Ma and my aunts can't make them as well as you. And that's incredible.' I stroked the embroidery of Lord Ganesh, admiring the Lord's delicate crown, the jovial smile, and the trunk curved just so. 'I don't think I can do such a fine job even with my water colours,' I said with conviction, 'And needlework requires more patience and precision.'

'I know you like this,' Pishi said. 'You can keep it and remember me through it after I die.'

'Don't talk about dying, Pishi.' I hugged her and breathed deeply, yearning to hold on to her scent of coconut oil with a hint of incense forever. And then I talked to her, of school, of life back home in Delhi. 'I've only told this to Baba and my best friend, Vinita.' I held Pishi tighter and prayed for her blessings. 'I'm studying for the entrance tests to medical colleges next year. Please don't tell the others yet. I don't know if I'll ever make it, but I want to become a doctor someday.'

Pishi placed her hands upon my head and muttered a prayer. Her lips trembled as she wiped her eyes with the corner of her sari. Holding her shrivelled hand, I thought of the opportunities she never had. I would never again take the benefits of my time for granted.

The brats ran in and joined us under the bed. They pushed a red tin bus on the floor and shouted 'Vroom! Vroom!' hoping to draw our attention. Then they tugged at my hands. I groaned inwardly at this distraction, and hoped they wouldn't torment me the way they did during my last visit. The girl put her arms around me and shyly handed me a page torn from a notebook. It was scrawled over with crayon drawings of flowers, butterflies, and a lopsided elephant. 'To Mithu Didi,' it said in rainbow hues. 'With love from Nina and Pintu.'

'Eat your rosogollas, dear.' Pishi sat up and ran her knobby fingers through my hair. The kids sat around me with wide, wistful eyes like a pair of kittens. Did they want rosogollas? I picked up one rosogulla—warm and dripping with rose-scented sugar syrup—as they watched and shied away. I held Nina's dimpled hand and placed a round white rosogolla in her palm. Then, I pulled Pintu onto my lap and popped one right into his pink little mouth. Pintu smiled and Nina planted a syrupy kiss on my cheek.

From now on, I would remember their names.

My aunt came and called me to the sitting room again. Baba had been eyeing his watch for a while, and Ma finally conceded that it was time to leave. My aunt handed me two gift-wrapped boxes and whispered, 'Open these with your cousin after you reach home.' She also gave me an earthen pot full of warm, freshly-made rosogollas for Tukuda.

Many handshakes, hugs, and respectful feet touching later, we left with promises of another visit and invitations for everyone to stay with us in Delhi. Pishi packed some preserves and nadus just for me.

'I'll come again next year, and we'll talk of many more things,' I told her. I squeezed Pishi's hand and silently prayed that she would still be with us.

Baba, in a fit of extravagance, hired a taxi all the way to our base in Tukuda's house. I looked out of the taxi's window and waved back at the family assembled in their balcony to see us off.

'Come again, Mithu Didi,' Nina cried out.

'Don't go!' Pintu shouted. My aunt patted him as he sobbed in her arms.

The cityscape was transformed by darkness. Bright lights created haloes around storefront displays and lamp posts. The shadows hid the peeling plaster and broken windows.

I stroked our presents and wished Tukuda had come along. We could have laughed away the jolting bus ride, and Pishi's scrapbook of newspaper clippings would have impressed him. I balanced the pot of rosogollas on my lap and pictured Tukuda's excitement at the gifts and sweets. The rosogollas would get cold by the time we reached their house. It wouldn't be the same as sharing them fresh and warm in Pishi's room.

No Return Address!

Manjira Majumdar

We leave something of ourselves behind when we leave a place, we stay there, even though we go away. And there are things in us that we can find again only by going back there.
—Pascal Mercier, *Night Train to Lisbon*

The strong whiff of *bidi* from the verandah indicated that my uncle or *jethamoshai* (elder brother of my father) was visiting us. Back from school, we would sit down to lunch, and he would join us in his white *fatua* (collarless shirt) and white *lungi* worn in the South Indian style. He would wolf down the mound of rice like someone who had not had a good meal for a long time. A well would be dug into the rice, as he punctured it, and poured copious amount of the pale yellow *daal* into it.

'Is there any *ghee*?' he would ask my mother, in a sort of a voice that bespoke of entitlement. 'Is there anything else you want—salt, chili?' my mother would enquire politely.

Every family has a black sheep, and he was ours. The person you want to hide from society and never speak about, ever.

My uncle, a bachelor, was a vagabond of sorts. We never addressed him as *jethu*—the shorter and more affectionate term. There was nothing loveable about him. With big ears sticking out, something that my sister when very young, always made fun of—he possessed a prominent Fagin-like nose as seen in the musical *Oliver Twist* and had a lean figure.

His aristocratic look was camouflaged under a weathered tan of fair skin that had seen better days. He roamed from town to town, sometimes cities, doing odd jobs and smoking his cheap hand-rolled *bidi*, the smell of which, my father who was a connoisseur of the good things in life, detested.

From bits of conversation I heard, *jethamoshai* wrote application letters in English for jobs, as there were many refugees like him—looking for an opening in many of the British mercantile firms that flourished in Kolkata then. He also visited many of my mother's relatives, who are from this side of Bengal, and after accepting their hospitality, bad mouthed them. He caused considerable embarrassment to my father.

Life meandered like a long, winding road as we grew up. We were too young to understand all this! Life, back then, promised beautiful surprises hiding under those polka-dotted toad stools of our English picture books—a life that was yet to come.

But when *jethamoshai* showed up at our doorstep, it spelt bad news. The atmosphere kind of soured. He quarreled with everyone and often overturned his plate of rice in anger. He scuttled all our enjoyment plans. Yet, when he was in a better mood, which was rare, he brought expensive fruits and candies for us, his nephew and nieces. Having earned some money, he exhibited it by the two sets of clean white *dhoti* and *kurta* he stuffed into his worn duffel bag, with one handle almost coming off.

On some afternoons he told us stories, sometimes his hands touching my sister and me inappropriately. One story that he loved to narrate was that when he was returning from his village school one day, an Englishman, probably a soldier, asked him, 'Hey boy do you know the name of this village?' to which, he answered, '*Eta Pangsha* (This is Pangsha)' the name of their village. Then, the guy pointed to the other side (I think the rail tracks) and asked, 'And that one?' The boy replied, '*Shetao Pangsha* (That too!)'

The soldier then commented, 'Oh I see! This place is

known as Etapangsha and that place Shetapangsha.' This went on for some time before the misunderstanding was cleared between this *(eta)* and that *(sheta)*. The story may have been a borrowed one. We continue to narrate it at gatherings even today and laugh till tears stream down our faces. The tears now sting my eyes like bees and have a terrible salty taste to it. Do I forgive this man's many transgressions? I don't really know.

Jethamoshai came alive through pale yellow postcards. In the absence of a telephone, they were the cheapest form of communication in those days. He constantly wrote letters from all over the place, always asking about my father's well-being and always ending with news that he would come around soon to visit us. Letters in those days were never thrown away. Postcards were given to young boys going out into the world to study or work, to write letters back home.

Refugee families wrote postcards under trees, sometimes *en route* to some destination, not having a roof over their heads, so these had no return addresses! It was very late in life that I learnt this. My father would marvel at my uncle's beautiful handwriting and compared his well-formed letters to pearls. The post marks showed some railway or colliery colony, in which lived members of my father's extended family, including cousins and their families. Strangely, each postcard had a return address I found out later.

So even if a post card signaled that he was still alive, it also meant that it was time for him to move again, the restless wanderer that he was. He would make a short visit to us in between, which Baba instinctively knew was for monetary assistance. So the postcards continued to come and pile up inside a transparent plastic bag, some frayed at the edges; the ink gradually faded so the letters peered like tiny insects crawling inside, crying to be set free.

It happened on a day when we were playing hopscotch. My young friends who spied someone approaching, all scattered away squealing, 'Pagol Pagol' Madman... madman. Run...run.

I turned around to see it was *jethomoshai!* In rag tag clothes, a scraggy beard, he scared the hell out of me. And just to show I didn't know him, I too ran away and hid in my neighbor's flat.

He came home and my mother gave him a clean set of clothes; never ever mean with food, she cooked him an elaborate meal, which he ate with great relish. He wanted to leave before my father came back from office as he knew his younger brother would be terribly angry.

So after resting a bit, he asked my mother for some cash, which she kept hidden in her *puja* altar for emergencies, and taking the amount, he quickly departed. He told her he had found some nice job. For life, was all about hope and something to that effect!

We were happy to see him go. When my father came

home, sniffed and uttered turning up his nose, '*Dada* (elder brother) must have been here.' That's all!

Among his other talents, made fun of by my witty Baba, was that he also sold bits of family artifacts on the sly, but what the rest of his family could not forgive him for was that he misplaced the deed of their old house, especially when it was needed the most, for some sort of exchange of property. He never lived up to the stature of an elder brother, who took care of the family. In between his sobs, Baba was saying something about a beautiful *chatim* tree bower, rightly known as blackboard tree, which shaded a stage, which many well-off East Bengali homes had, where they put up plays and musical soirees, often young men dressed in drags. He would direct amateur plays, teach them songs composed by DL Roy and elocution, something that Baba was almost a professional at. There was not much money—there was heartache, but there was also love and laughter and hope for the future.

His elder brother read out Bengali classics or translations of world classics to his younger siblings and several cousins. And told them about the world that lay beyond the village or whatever he made of it. He took them to village fairs. He was moderately good in studies, had mastered English quite well.

But for years *jethamoshai* did not show up at all! We just caught snatches of conversation that he was spotted here and there. And suddenly one day, we received news that he had passed away at a sort of a home.

One late night, many years later I woke up to my father's loud sobs. He was remembering his Dada so full of eccentricities, yet full of life when he was growing up, even without a formal male guardian.

Baba was perhaps crying about the life he dreamed he could have had compared to the one he had. His family, in a way, washed away like driftwood, bit by bit. Yet it was not such a bad life in the city of this part of Bengal. The invisible pain was elsewhere; perhaps a certain loss and longing for it to be made good.

Baba and his family came as penniless refugees from across the eastern border of India, more precisely from Faridpur in the Rajbari district of Dhaka Division. All these words like erstwhile East Pakistan and now Bangladesh, and West Bengal are mere nomenclatures in the face of the human tragedy, which I am still trying to piece together. What I once considered historical, political or geographical issues are perceived through the prism of grief, loss, rootlessness and personal history laced with indignation. We realize the mistakes that were committed—mistakes that affected the Bengali transgeneration—in more ways than we would like to think.

By the time my Baba was born, their family *zamindari* was already in tatters. He had lost his own father when he was four years old—a fact that bothered him all his life—even more than the Partition. More than land, the family once with interests in indigo, had to sell off land and a pond or two—to support a very decadent lifestyle!

At least that's what Ma said. Baba did occasionally mention the silver betel nut cases strewn around the house, rare Persian (court language since the Moghul days) texts, exquisite *jamewar* (Kashmiri) shawls and rare pieces of jewellery, which my grandmother had brought in as her dowry. These my uncle later sold facetiously, sometimes, even surreptitiously.

So whatever pride they had—still owning vast tracts of land, with a crumbling house but a house that was standing nevertheless, was smashed to smithereens overnight when they had to flee, fearing the security of women. When they came, their status was turned on its head!

From *babuder barir lok* (men of the manor), respected by their many Muslim retainers, overnight they were rendered homeless. They did not know where their next meal would come from. The shards of glass remained broken, never to be made whole again.

That my Baba was totally amnesiac regarding this sudden and chaotic transition from one region to another, not very different in fauna, flora and language, did not help matters. He spoke about it in fits and starts, despite being very articulate and talkative.

I think like most people who hide a deep secret pain

within, he too would skirt around the issue—of so many other things, except that one thing that made him what he was!

He was a refugee—a displaced person. There were several other descriptive terms, none too complimentary. His identity was reduced to a piece of paper. He complained if the rice was over boiled, he complained if the fish was undercooked but he never complained about the Partition. And every Bengali middle class *bhadrolok* was similar in many ways.

We children, consisting of me, my elder brother and younger sister were never conscious of our Bengali identity leave alone an East Bengali one. Growing up in a neighbourhood near Chowringhee, we meshed in with the cosmopolitan locality. In fact, Bengalis were conspicuous by their absence in the central business district anyway. They only came to work in the various government offices within the vicinity, which included Dalhousie, or to shop in New Market.

I recall the members of several Left parties, poets and writers weaving in and out of the house. So Partition was not such a bad deal, after all. Baba's wide networking through the party activities helped him and my two uncles and aunt to get employment despite their modest educational qualifications. That my uncle frequently quit his job is another story! My mother was quite fed up with this impoverished and eccentric family.

She belonged to a landed family of Bashirhat, and grew up in a big house on the banks of the lazy Icchamoti River, except when it was in spate. She, however, stood by my father through thick and thin, even helping those people more unfortunate than them.

One of the last post cards that came from *jethamoshai* was when my parents went to USA to meet my brother. He had mentioned in detail how they were to carry extra woolen garments since it was going to be a long plane journey and took at least two days because of the distance—claiming they needed to carry some extra food in *tiffin* carriers. He was totally out of touch with reality, confusing a train journey with a journey on the plane. He was old with still some care left to bestow.

Jethamoshai always lived between two worlds—the real and the unreal—we had no clue to the latter. By the time the last of the post cards came, he was already quite ill, and in the last stages of his life. His skin had lost its sheen and had become dark and scaly according to my younger uncle or *Kaku* who tracked him down. He was in some dismal room in some sort of a home, we were told. He was still asking for money, again in the way of entitlement. His handwriting was still legible demonstrating a lucid mind. He passed away soon after in the arms of strangers who cared for him.

The last postcard had no return address.

Everyone was secretly relieved when he died. Many

years later, at one of my cousin's wedding, I recall, a distant relative enquired loudly for everyone to hear, 'Was that mad uncle of yours ever found?' It stabbed my heart.

I couldn't tell him that his last days were spent sitting on the bed, not sleeping. And when he was asked to lie down, he would say, 'Can't you see Ma and *Didi* (elder sister) lying there? They need rest after the long trek across the border!' Grandmother had passed away a long, long ago and so had my aunt. He still displayed some affection and concern but no one got to see or feel it.

Jethu died almost a vagrant. But then again, he lived on his own terms, ruling that laying down roots anywhere would prove futile. When we shifted to a new, much smaller place after Baba's retirement, his bundle of postcards was thrown away, like other unwanted papers. Already brittle like cookies, they scattered away like crumbs of faded memories, but the painful scabs remained forever.

Years had passed since *Jethamoshai* had crossed the border. But his subconscious mind still trapped him there during his last days, as he kept muttering *etapangsha otapangsha*. Weren't we all stuck in that one moment? Did Baba also revisit the moment he became rootless? His roots twisted and jerked with a snap of someone else's finger. Now with my father and his siblings gone, I can compare them to the brown leaf detached from its tree on a dark autumn day, still hovering in the air. Were they also waiting to return to their land to plant their roots again?

The realization of my own loss, identity, roots and home has only thrown more questions at me than answers. Perhaps, I will never completely understand the scars on our collective psyche.

It is often our souls that have no return address!

Alam's Own House
Dibyendu Palit

Now the Dhaka sky was behind him. The 'Bangladesh Biman Boeing' straightened out, nose towards Calcutta. Other thoughts cropped up in his mind, 'Like everything else, there comes a moment of return. When that slips away, it's impossible to ever be back,' Raka had written in her last letter.

'I feel that's what will happen to you. Of course, I'm not tired of waiting for you, nor am I feeling low. All this is just to say – come when you can, warning shots are quite unnecessary.' Impossible to remember words like these, and many more, in all this time.

Alamer Nijer Bari written by Dibyendu Palit has appeared in *Mapmaking: Partition Stories from two Bengals (Amaryllis)* and has been translated by Debjani Sengupta,

It struck Alam that the Calcutta parlance – ambiguities and all – had finally got to Raka after years in the city. She knew how to hide behind words now. Alam had not understood the intent of her words when she wrote, '*That* particular soil in which we take root.'

He had read the line over and over again – his doubts had to be dispelled. There was no room for them. But really, he had no clue. He had worried over the letter. Raka was a woman, after all. She ought to have behaved like one. Did traditions get wiped out the moment one gained independence? There were things to be grasped, meanings to be comprehended. On the other hand, Alam may have misunderstood, in that case, Raka was under no obligation to explain.

So he had replied:

Your reproach is a riddle. If it is your resentment that speaks, then I understand. Otherwise, there are many things in your letter the meaning of which have escaped me. What do you mean, 'that particular soil in which we take root?' If it means what I think it means, don't forget I was born in Calcutta – in the very house in Park Circus where this letter is to be delivered. So aren't I rooted in Calcutta? Do you know, there are more girls named Raka here, than in Calcutta, and the name sits on them just fine! Until you come to Dhaka, Alam will keep running to Calcutta, to his own house…'

Words like these – and then some! – possible only in letters. Yet language too, had the capacity to put words together and sculpt the sense, render them in flesh and blood, make them mean. Such were his feelings Alam would gladly have been his own messenger.

There was no reply. Alam wrote again after a month, just a few lines. He wrote about not receiving a reply and of having been invited to Calcutta on a Friendship Committee Seminar.

Raka must realize, men hurt too.

The reply, when it came, had the address written by another hand. He slipped the letter out of the envelope and unfolded the paper. Yes, he was right. It was Sneha mashima, not Raka. To begin with, Raka was not in Calcutta. When at home, she in any case kept too busy with her research to write letters. Alam must write and keep in touch. Lastly, Meshomashai was very happy at the news of his seminar, etcetra, etcetra. . . .

It was clear that Raka didn't know her mother had written. Nevertheless, he tried to rationalize. The university remained closed in May-June, and they had relatives all over the country. Beginning from 1946, the various branches of the family had spread to all corners of the country – Delhi, Pune, Patna, Ahmedabad. Raka loved to travel. She might have left for any of these places at a moment's notice. It was not possible to restrain her just with letters. How could Alam ask either Raka or

Sneha mashima to explain?

As a whiff of cigarette smoke teased his nostrils, Alam realized how heavily he was breathing. He tried to shift in his seat. The flight was a short one – a mere forty-five minutes. The plane didn't even need to climb thousands of feet. It flew so low that if one looked down one saw the world below in snatches – hazy trees, fields, rivers, concrete structures.

Now the plane began to roll. The blue sky gave way to clouds.

Alam felt the change in the cabin temperature. It was August end, monsoon, perhaps there was a storm outside. At that instant, the bell rang and lights came on – time to fasten seatbelts – then the stewardess's warning voice. Beside him Feroz, smoking, was leafing through his seminar paper. He shut the lid of his briefcase and asked, 'Have we reached already?'

'Another fifteen minutes,' replied Alam. 'Lots of bumps on a low flight like this.' As he spoke, the plane entered a wall of thick clouds. Thankfully, there weren't too many jolts. In a few moments, they could see the sky again, clearer now, and not grey at all.

'This sky belongs to India,' said Feroz, as the warning sign went off. 'We have no – how should I put it – citizen's right over it.' Alam looked at him. Off hand, he couldn't think of anything to say.

Jesting tone apart, it was obvious that Feroz was

serious. No sooner had he accepted the invitation to the seminar, that he had begun to grapple with the topic. There had to be an adversary – without an enemy his arguments would have no feet to stand on. They had argued till late the night before. Feroz believed that the cultural identities of the two countries were separate. He had said, 'Friendship is fine, but it is dangerous to use it as bait. We wear clothes to hide our nakedness, but why must the colour and cut be the same? What of our individuality?' Alam did not think like that, 'Difference in cut and colour? Probably, Feroz meant something deeper, but it was not even clear to himself.'

And here he was, once again moving towards the 'Us and Them' topic. 'What do you mean?' Alam retorted. 'If we had the time and the patience, we could have walked the distance. Things would be much simpler then. Where there is no distance, there is no need of a seminar on friendship.' 'What do you mean?' asked Feroz.

'I took the opportunity because I wanted to come to Calcutta,' Alam continued. 'Otherwise all this "seminaring" is just pretence. One language, one dress, same food and climate – the difference is only political. What else can one say?'

'Don't finish off a two-day seminar in five minutes. I've slogged for six nights on my paper,' Feroz parried, as if playing for time. Then vehemently, 'The difference is not simply political. It is of religion. Can you deny that even if you want to?'

It seemed to Alam that the plane was on its way down. Such moments were hushed. A silence descended upon people, a stillness. He didn't want to speak now, he would be overheard. Any other time, he would have replied, 'Religion is imposed. As a fad, it is blind and therefore, easy to believe in. We have never understood the relation between the rich and the poor, or between the exploited and the exploiter, but we seem to understand the binds of religion. It is irresponsible and makes it easy to escape reality.'

'But', he said, 'Was there a point to all this? Some questions were unanswerable, and often, one was too tired to argue.

'Was it possible that what he had felt, the thoughts and doubts that had swirled in his head during the flight, were also those that occurred to Raka? Or was language merely an array of alphabets or empty forms? Was feeling reducible to merely a touch of the *narayanshila*? The questions nagged him.

He knew Raka's mind, but not all of it.

Feroz would, of course, disagree. He was built differently. Now he was sitting upright, ready for the landing. He started off on another subject. 'Alam, will you really not stay with me?'

'I've already told you they would feel bad if I did not stay with them.' 'You can visit them,' retorted Feroz. A pause, and then he said, 'These people you talk about, they are not even relatives.'

'Am I related to you? But if I ever leave Dhaka, I'll stay with you when I visit –'

The conversation got lost in the bustle of landing. Pushing past the milling crowd and walking down the steps, Alam took it up again. 'You won't be alone. It's just for a night, and Rahman Saheb will be there tomorrow morning, and Khan Choudhury of the Mission, too.'

Feroz didn't reply.

It seemed to have rained a while ago. A wet wind eddied around while a mild sun tried to mop up the moist air. Moving towards the Customs enclosure, a hazy memory brushed past Alam, softly. Three years ago he had walked the other way on this very tarmac. Moving towards the waiting aircraft, his eyes had searched the visitors' gallery for Raka. She was there, and so were Sneha mashima and Ananta meshomoshai. He hadn't spotted them immediately. In a sea of faces waiting to say goodbye, it was difficult to pick them out. But a pale hand waving among the dense mass had shown Raka to him. He hadn't been able to bear the sight. Even after the plane had taken off, that farewell had haunted him. Today, he thought again about the distance – forty-five minutes, perhaps an hour away. It had taken him three long years to cross it.

The strength of the memory made him cast a glance

at the gallery. Not to look for Raka, just a lingering query. A week ago he had sent two similarly worded letters, one to Raka and the other to Sneha mashima, mentioning his flight number and time of arrival.

Two letters; because he wished to remain true to his reasons, and not because he thought one of them might get lost. Nobody had Calcutta for an address! He had wanted to make it clear that, from the airport, he would go to Park Circus. What else could he have written? Perhaps Raka would remember that morning that Alam's address was Calcutta not Dhaka!

The thought cheered him up. Raka wasn't there, even so his eyes skimmed over the crowd around him. Khan Choudhury was there to receive them, along with two others from the Friendship Committee. Alam recognized Sudeb Basu. He had come to Dhaka the previous year on a similar seminar, but everything was cancelled because of the death of Zia-ur-Rehman. On the way to the city Sudeb launched into the story with great gusto. Feroz and Alam knew it well, so did Khan Choudhury, maybe the fourth member was listening in. In a short while, Sudeb changed back and launched forth on the Partition. He stated that thousands had crossed over to India, but when he began to theorize about the actual number Feroz interrupted and started picking holes in the statistics. It seemed to Alam that the entire seminar had begun in the car itself!

Irritated, Alam said, 'Feroz, give me a cigarette –'

'Why, suddenly?'

'I have come here after three years, I just feel like celebrating!' Sudeb stopped speaking and turned to look at Alam, 'You know Calcutta, don't you?'

Trying to light his cigarette with shaky hands, Alam said, 'I was born here.' At that instant, he found it easy to hide within himself.

The question whether the country of one's birth was also one's motherland always awakened a sense of rootlessness in him; as it did now.

They talked about the 1971 war. Calcutta was mad about Sheikh Mujib. Sudeb babu began to talk of a meeting that had been held under the Monument – Suchitra Mitra had sung to the crowds. Alam suddenly remembered that he had been in Calcutta then. It was in that meeting that for the first time he had heard the newly announced name of a country—whose stamp of citizenship he now carried.

After a little while the sky changed colour. A drizzle began, accompanied by a gusty damp wind. It was good to sit next to the window; the assailing wind could play around one's face. They crossed Nazrul Islam Avenue and came to C.I.T. Road—to the left, the road led to Salt Lake, then Maniktala, Narkeldanga. It was like the roll call in class, one knew all the familiar faces.

A tremor ran through Alam's body. He wanted to take a taxi and renew his acquaintance with these names, but Khan Choudhury wouldn't let him. The driver would first drop Feroz at his hotel and then take him to Park Circus. It was Saturday, eleven in the morning and it would be almost twelve by the time he reached. If his letter had reached, Raka would be waiting. The fragrance of the *kathalichampa* near the gate would have spread in the moist air.

And if the letter had not reached, she would be surprised. The Raka he had known three years ago must have changed. Maybe Alam would also be taken by surprise. They might argue whether the *ilish* from the Ganga were better than those from the Padma. Possibly Ananta meshomashai would be taken aback to find that Alam was still a fan of the fish from this part of the border and not the other. 'Taste is like tradition', he had once said. 'Once you acquire it, you can tolerate any indignity for its sake.'

If on that day or the next – while staying with them – Alam said something similar regarding Raka, would Ananta meshomoshai be very surprised? Or Sneha mashima? Alam kept to his thoughts. It was rude to be silent when others were talking, but the tide of memory was strong.

1970

Suddenly Baba decided to give up his practice. The chamber closed – unless it was an emergency, he stopped going out on calls. He wasn't ill, and he had had a roaring practice. It was grief accumulated over the years. Only later did Alam get to know of it.

A year before that, Dada had left to study engineering in Glasgow. 'You'll get a job there, although you may feel impoverished in your mind,' Baba had advised. 'Don't come back, if you can.' Many things that he had said then were puzzling, difficult to understand.

Sitting in his empty chamber Baba would explain his theories about the world to his compounder. There were two Partitions – one political, the other in the mind. Mountbatten had not put his signature to the second. Earlier, the same stethoscope would be used on Ram and Jamal. But those days were past. 'Now, among my patients there is no Ram, only Jamal, no Kanai, only Karim. Ram, Kanai, Jadu have all gone to Dr Gupta. We were students together in the Medical College, learnt the same anatomy from the same cadaver. Those bodies did not wear name tags.'

Alam clearly remembered how Baba would sit down to eat, a large copper plate piled high with rice, and chat with Ma. Sitting there, he broke the news one day. Dr Gupta had acquired a chamber in Ballygunge as he had very few patients left in this part of the town. 'Jamals and Karims come to me. Even their numbers are dwindling. People are leaving for Pakistan, either east or west. Shouldn't we go too? I can feel a sickness welling up in me …'

So many years had elapsed—Alam couldn't remember the words too well. But he did remember Baba's quiet face, pinched and lonely—Ma, who slowly fell silent—the sorrows of his young sisters, in that pimply age when everything was a catastrophe—the dim glow of a melancholy light bulb. And then the war began—Bangladesh, Oh my Bangladesh!

The proposal came from Dr Gupta. Anantashekhar had to leave Dhaka with his family. He had no wish to go back and he had left behind a house and farmland in Dhanmondi. 'Weren't you planning to leave, Doctor? I thought I ought to advise you. If you are serious about leaving, why don't you both exchange your properties?'

Baba looked grim. Later he said, 'If that is what Fate has in store for us, then so be it. Let me see. Bring Anantababu along one of these days.' Feroz got off, so did Khan Chowdhury and the others. The plans for the day were changing, some more people would join them. There was to be a dinner. Khan Chowdhury requested his presence.

Alam nodded, but he didn't know if he could be there. As soon as the car left the hotel portico, an uneasy solitude engulfed him. Why was he trying to be alone? Was it for one-way memories? Now that his destination drew near, doubts clamoured in his mind.

Alam really didn't know. Right now, all he recognized

were the questions that stood between him and the house he was going to. In three years, Calcutta had changed. He was so busy trying to guess how much Raka might have changed—his own transformation had escaped him. When we stand in front of the mirror, the face we see in it seems so familiar. Our eyes are not accustomed to noticing yesterday's changes. The present merges into the past as our minds, too, change course. Our new face and soul can only be discerned by someone for whom time has separated the past and the present.

Alam realized that the roads in that area were never so pockmarked, the walls so full of slogans – 'Power comes from the barrel of a gun' – somewhat faded. The black ink on the walls seemed to leap up from the holes strewn across the roads. Humans were like roads too – all the comings and goings changed them – it was not possible to know how much at a glance. The day Dr. Gupta brought Anantashekhar home, Alam realized how much Baba had changed. Baba spoke courteously, but without his usual warmth, 'I've been told of the exchange. Have you got plans and lists for your property in Dhaka?'

'Sorry,' Anantasekhar replied. 'I have just the plan for my house. I can give you a rough estimate.'

'Rough estimates won't do.' Baba looked directly at Anantasekhar. 'Listen, Anantababu, I've made up my mind. Look over my house today. If you like it, we can take this ahead. Then let's go to Dhaka – I'll take a look at your house. This house has been built with my blood. It had taken four years to build, and is the first two-storey building in this area. Look at the terrace – it's as big as a courtyard. After Mahatmaji was assasinated, we held a condolence meeting here. I felt curiously empty when the meeting broke up. In the cold winter night, standing on the new terrace, I saw how immense the sky was…'

Alam had asked the driver to move slowly so that he could direct him – now right, now left. His eyes looked for familiar sights and found only novelty. This single storey house had sprouted another floor. That flowering garden was almost obliterated by the rudeness of a motor-garage while a new signboard proclaimed how expendable the old one was. But he had no trouble recognizing his old house. There never would be. 'I'm the only person who has been born in the same house twice,' Alam had once told Raka. At least that was what he had thought then.

The exchange happened very quickly, within two months. But Alam remained behind. It was his final year in MA. He had argued long and hard with himself before making up his mind – if Baba wanted to leave, it was his decision, why must he drag Alam too?

'Where will you stay?' Baba asked. 'Find a hostel then.' Sitting in his own house, this discussion in front of Anantasekhar shook Alam.

'Alam will stay where he is,' Anantasekhar interrupted. 'If he leaves with you, well, that is different. But if he's in

Calcutta, he can't possibly stay anywhere else. Besides,' Anantasekhar's face shone even as he spoke in the face of Baba's silence, 'Doctor Saheb, I started the whole thing, not you. You gave me shelter, can't I do the same for your son now! Besides, I have a son too! They can stay together…'

'You reassure me,' Baba replied. 'You know, once bitten, twice shy. Didn't we co-exist once? One never spoke of an infliction then, did one? Then why this uneasiness now, this torment? Thank God, the exchange has taken place. I understand why you want to help my son. I just hope you don't regret it.' Crossing the border, at the crack of dawn, before leaving for the station, Baba offered *namaz* on the terrace for the last time.

As he went out, he didn't even look back once. Following him down the stairs, Alam thought, continuity manifested itself in man's blood, not where he lived.

Alam's room was on the terrace. Even after the house changed hands, Alam stayed in the same room. One evening Raka came up, panting, 'Dada called – there's chaos outside, houses are being burnt down – you're not to go out anywhere.' Raka's expression at that moment was more precious than her words. Without masking his surprise, Alam said, 'You're wearing a sari today?' Raka looked at herself. Her alarm forgotten, she asked, 'Do I look awful?' Terms of endearment were always neutral, Alam thought. That which the eye didn't see was precisely what it gazed upon. He couldn't explain this to Raka. He looked at her, and tried to tell her, but didn't. Standing on the terrace next to Raka, he saw the fiery glow spreading like a livid wound in the distance. Cries of anguish were inseparable from those of the attackers, from a distance they sounded as if they erupted from the same throat. Then, everything fell silent. A while later, Raka exclaimed, 'It's happening here too!' Alam didn't utter a word. Suddenly, he thought how insignificant that moment was, the two of them standing side by side, like puppets, nothing more. And when a busy Sneha mashima called Raka away, he thought no more of it.

'Hey, stop!'

The car stopped abruptly, and Alam exhaled the air he had kept locked in his chest. Suitcase in hand, he stepped out of the car. But before he let the driver go, he wanted to make sure the house was the same. He asked himself if there was any reason for doubt. He could clearly see the marble nameplate on the wall next to the small gate – Anantasekhar Sanyal. Within a month of Baba's departure, the old one had been removed. It was necessary as patients often came knocking at the door, refusing to believe that Doctor Saheb had left the country forever. Without sentimentality, Alam had suggested it himself.

No, it wasn't that. He didn't recognize the house because the *kanthalichampa* had vanished; in its place stood a concrete structure – a sweetshop called 'Madhur'. The house used to be instantly recognisable; people knew it as the house with the *kanthalichampa* tree. Perhaps they now knew it by the shop's name. Raka never wrote about these changes – surely there was a reason.

'The house is big but not too many rooms ...' Anantasekhar had once remarked, 'Incorrect planning'. Alam had smiled to himself. If Baba had heard that before the exchange, he would have refused to go ahead. He had planted the tree so that it would be visible from the bedroom upstairs and the sitting room below. No reason to tell Anantasekhar meshomoshai all that. Perhaps he wanted to utilize the open space. Necessity taught men their habits. The car left, but Alam continued to stand in front of the gate. He looked at the house and saw Baba at the bedroom window, in his check cloth lungi and loose undershirt. The slightly reddish beard, covering his chin, was lit with a cloudy light. It was raining over the *kanthalichampa* tree. Alam's breath caught in his throat – was it a faint fragrance he could smell? It was the yellow curtain billowing in the wind, it wasn't Baba. The drops of rain on his face brought him back to the present. Alam looked up at the sky—clouds. He remembered how it had rained all the way from the airport. He wondered if he was being sentimental, the way he kept going back to the past. Crossing the gate, he ascended the steps, reached the verandah, and then the door. The moment he rang the bell, it would open. Raka? No, he had no hopes. Perhaps Sneha mashima, or Meshomashai would open it.

He waited, and pressed the bell switch again. It wasn't too late – just past noon. Anyway, they knew he was coming.

The door opened. Sneha mashima, with her right hand half hidden—she had been having her lunch. With a glance half-awkward, half-surprised, she exclaimed, 'Oh Alam!'

In his old manner, Alam bent forward to touch her feet and asked, 'Did you get my letter?'

'Come in.' Sneha mashima refused to answer directly. 'I was eating – sit.' Alam put the suitcase in a corner. The room was packed with chairs. He glanced at the curtain that separated the room from the dining space, and his heart sank.

'Mashima, please have your lunch. I'll wait.'

'Alright.' A faint smile floated on her lips. 'Your Meshomashai will finish in a moment.'

She threw a quick look at the suitcase and asked, 'Will you have some tea?'

'Yes. But after you've had your lunch.'

'Why don't you sit?'

Three years ago Alam would have unhesitatingly walked in the door Sneha had now disappeared through. Raka had always opened the front door to let him in, in the evenings. That was the time he usually returned. Now, there hung a yellow curtain. This time perhaps, when the curtain parted, it would be Raka. He had nothing to do but wait. Deliberately, Alam kept his mind blank.

The picture of Gandhi still hung on the wall to the right. It had been brought down on the night of the condolence meeting. Alam remembered the picture from the time he was three or four. On the wall opposite were the mounted horns of an antelope. But an empty space mutely testified to the absent oil painting of Alam's great grandfather. He had fought in the Battle of Plassey, next to Mohanlal, and his descendants had lived in Murshidabad. The painting had hung in their Behrampur house and had traveled to Calcutta with Baba. Alam had effortlessly remembered that history while scattering the loose dry soil at Baba's grave in Dhaka. Now, looking at the antelope horns, he thought of nothing else.

'How are you Alam?' asked Anantasekhar. The question came even before he entered the room.

'I'm fine. But you don't look too good.'

Alam bent to touch his feet. 'Why? Have I lost weight?'

'Yes.'

'I don't keep well these days.'

The undershirt was greyer than the dhoti – perhaps Anantasekhar had just worn whatever had come to hand. He now opened the window near the road and came to sit on the sofa.

'How's your mother – sisters?'

Alam nodded. Sneha came back. Was she wearing a different sari now? Alam was still preoccupied. He couldn't remember what colour she had worn earlier.

'We heard you were coming,' Anantasekhar spoke as if waking from deep thought.

'Why didn't you say you'd put up here?'

'What are you saying?' Sneha hurriedly broke in, even before he finished asking the question.

'When he's in Calcutta, where else can he stay?' Sneha was so clear about it that Anantasekhar looked a little embarrassed. Hesitantly, he said, 'I didn't mean anything ...'

'Come Alam. You'll wash?' Sneha quickly tried to rescue the situation. 'Tea will be ready ...'

Alam stood up. Following Sneha into the house he thought three years had been a long time, long enough to destroy spontaneity. Or was it even more? It was also possible that his letters were not shown to Anantasekhar – with the forgetfulness of age, something else might have happened to him. It was also Alam's responsibility to see that everything was as natural as before. Sneha had hung fresh towels and put in a new soap case. Handing it to Alam she said, 'Will you take a bath?'

'No. I had one in the morning.'

'Have lunch. Then rest a little' As if to a stranger,

Sneha showed the way.

'That's the bathroom. We've put in new fittings. You haven't forgotten, have you?'

Alam smiled. If it came to the count, Alam knew every nook and cranny of this house better than Sneha would ever do. Ownership was something else. Looking at his wet face in the mirror facing the washbasin, Alam thought that for him the bathroom *was* new. From the terrace, just eight steps led to the Second floor and the bathroom there. Alam had had the sole use of it; sometimes Srimantada used it, sometimes Raka. She once chided him lightly, 'Not even a son-in-law has this privilege – using the upstairs in splendid isolation while we share!'

Alam hadn't known then that the sudden news of Baba's death would make him give up his university job in Calcutta and leave for Dhaka. So he had replied in the same vein, 'It is best not to share. It will be even better if I got less love.' Raka had understood what he meant— the blush on her cheeks was proof enough. Recovering, she had retorted, 'People who talk big end up with nothing.'

The memory made him laugh. It brought back the entire scene so clearly that he could have touched Raka if he wanted to. But it also made him more anxious. Sitting down to lunch, Alam couldn't hide his misgivings. Sneha was doing all she could to make him comfortable. Her fussing and bustling hid what needed to be asked. The smoking plate showed she had cooked more rice while Alam was drinking his tea. The fried vegetables were an effort to fill the plate. Standing next to the dining table, she served Alam herself, and chatted brightly.

'Your old room is now a prayer room. After Srimanta was posted to Delhi, we converted his room to a guest room, though we hardly have anybody to stay over! Last month, my cousin's son came for an interview from Jalpaiguri.' Suddenly she stopped and exclaimed, 'Why aren't you eating? Aren't you hungry?'

'No, I am.'

Looking up, Alam met Sneha's eyes and waited, his patience at an end. Then he asked, 'Where's Raka? In college?'

'Oh, I completely forgot,' Sneha said, pouring water from the jug into a glass. 'Raka has gone to Delhi to see Srimanta. She's supposed to be back today, or tomorrow. She knows you're coming. The time is past now, so I think it will be tomorrow. It's so difficult to get tickets from Delhi …'

Looking down at his nearly empty plate, Alam began to push around the rest of the food. 'Which train is she taking? The Kalka Mail?'

'I think so.'

Alam couldn't think of anything more to say. The sound of a throat being cleared in the next room kept him quiet. Anantasekhar came in from the sitting room.

He pulled out a chair in front and said, 'I was told you're here for some seminar. What's the topic?'

The words hardly reached Alam's ears. He had no urge to reply. Glancing surreptitiously at his watch, he thought, Kalka Mail reached in the morning. When he lived in Calcutta, he had taken the same train to and from Delhi a couple of times for UGC interviews – he knew when it arrived at Howrah. If she was to arrive the day after, she must be in the train now. Another eighteen hours of waiting.

Alam's hands were still. The weight of hours oppressed his breath. Like heartache, it spread to all the empty spaces in his chest, stifling him. Thank God the following day was Sunday. There'd be enough time to wait. Perhaps he should ask if he could go to the station to receive her.

Anantasekhar was still waiting for Alam's reply, with his head on his hands. Light white stubble covered his cheeks and chin.

'It's a kind of cultural exchange,' Alam began. 'Discussing issues so that the people of the two countries can come closer, get to know each other …'

'Maybe that will happen.' Anantasekhar paused, and said almost to himself, 'But water and oil can never mix, can they? If they did, then your father would never have left Calcutta, and I would have stayed in Dhaka.' Anantasekhar spoke as if he knew exactly what to say to any question that might be put to him. Even in the midst of all his anguish, Alam wanted to laugh as he waited to see if Anantasekhar had anything more to say. He then replied, 'Meshomashai, we talk of the issue as that of oil and water because for years we have been taught to speak and think like that. But do we know which is the water and which the oil? Perhaps we'll find both are water, or both oil.'

'I don't understand!'

'There's no need to.' Sneha now interrupted, 'Why have you come to sit here? Let Alam be. He's tired. He needs to rest a bit.'

It was impossible to lessen eighteen hours by five or six minutes of conversation. One felt even more melancholic. Sneha mashima was right – weariness held him in its grip. If only he could fall off to sleep, and find the hours had gone by. What bliss!

Alam stood up. He tried to collect himself, then said, 'Mashima, I shan't be home for dinner.'

'Oh, but why?'

'I've promised them I'll be there. I'll be back late.'

Sneha looked steadily at Alam. Without meeting her eyes, Alam busied himself at the washbasin.

The room next to the sitting room was a guest room now. Sneha had described it. As soon as he lay down, sleep threatened to overtake him. He could feel it approaching, like a hurricane. Or was it at the speed of the Kalka Mail? Alam turned and laughed softly to himself. That was hardly a good simile to use. At that very moment it began to rain, large noisy drops.

Sneha woke him up.

'Didn't you have to go somewhere?' Alam realized it was evening. Or was it later than that? The rich wet smell of the earth blew in through the window but without the elusive fragrance of the *kanthalichampa*. It had stopped raining. Something was burning in his throat – was it because he had a late lunch? Sneha put on the light, and Alam looked at his watch; nearly seven. If only he had slept for thirteen more hours…

Alam stretched. 'How long I've slept Mashima! I'm a little late.'

Alam realized that Sneha was watching him intently. She moved away from him, and said, 'Get ready. I'll bring you tea.' It was Raka talking, she always used to say such things. Continuity remained, though now the threads were weak.

Walking towards the tram depot, the same thought buzzed in Alam's head. It was a grey, cloudy Saturday evening and buses and trams were empty. Also, he had come with only one address – that of his own house. When he tried to recollect other places he had known, his memory rushed past like sights seen from a train window. It was better to travel aimlessly, sit on a tram headed to Chowringhee, till it was time to be back. Then another wait, a few more hours, but that needn't be difficult. If sleep claimed him quickly, his distance with Raka would decrease just as rapidly.

Alam now realized that the emotion that always stirred in him when he thought of his own house had now converged—Raka had become all that the house once stood for.

When he tried to remember body, hands, feet, face he would only remember pliant windows, doors, stairs, and verandah! When he returned Sneha opened the door. Alam knew the guest room, the bathroom. Entering his room, he saw on the bedside table a neat arrangement – glass of water, a torch, a small bottle of betelnuts. Everything was tidily done and there was no reason to complain.

'Do you want anything more?'

'No.' Alam said, smiling.

'As soon as I sleep, it will be morning.'

'Doesn't your seminar start from Monday?'

Alam nodded. He wanted to say something, but didn't. He always awoke very early so he would say what he had planned to, in the morning. There was plenty of time left.

Sneha's eyes were still fixed on him. Alam said, 'Do you want to say something, Mashima?'

'No.'

Her voice sounded anxious. She collected herself,

and said, 'Go to bed, dear. I'm leaving.'

Alam switched off the light. He had slept well in the afternoon, but his body clamoured for rest. It was good, in a way. Yawning, he put his arms over his eyes. Half conscious now, he realised how the surrounding noises were becoming faint. Then sleep claimed him.

'Alam?'

The voice entered his consciousness and spread all over his body the tone familiar, the sensation new. Alam held back the reply. He took his time.

'Alam, are you asleep?'

'No, Mashima.'

'May I come in?'

Alam got up, switched on the light, drew back the curtain and let Sneha in.

'Is there something on your mind, Mashima?'

'No,' Sneha busied herself with the pillows. Putting aside the half-empty glass, she said, 'Be careful of cockroaches. The "pesticide people" were here a few days ago, but to no avail.'

Alam realized Sneha wasn't there to talk of pests. He hesitated, and then drew forward the chair.

'It was wonderful to have a meal cooked by you again.'

'You didn't eat much, a little fish and rice. We finish our shopping in the morning.'

Alam was silent and waited for her to say what she

had come to say.

'I couldn't tell you in front of Meshomashai …' Sneha blurted out in a different tone.

'Don't think poorly of us. If you've some plans regarding Raka, please forget them. It's my daughter's fault, she was wrong.'

Before Alam could react, she held out a letter that she had kept folded in her hand. 'Raka left it for you.'

Looking directly at her, Alam unfolded the piece of paper Raka had written:

> *I believed I was just as serious about you as you were about me. Then I received the last letter you sent me, and everything turned upside down. I questioned myself and I realized I had asked you to come here precisely because I knew you never would.*
>
> *Your intentions lie elsewhere – you want to uproot me. I am grateful to you, very grateful, but Alam, my will is weak. Somewhere, I am pulled back – somewhere, I am hurting! I don't know what it is. We had to change our addresses – this wall dispossessed us and many others too, before us. At the same time, we would never have come to know each other – nor indulged in this love, this pile-up of word upon word.*
>
> *You are an honest man. I couldn't say all this right to your face – so I ran away. The way I have put things are a little romantic, aren't they? Perhaps that's*

*because I do love you. Now I'm running away – far
from your love. The pain you will feel – I shall not.
Forgive me if you can. Keep in touch, if you want to.
If you write, I'll write back. We know some things
are a lie, but we do go on, don't we?*

Alam let go of his breath only after he reached the middle. Now, he folded the letter neatly and put it back in its envelope. A small piece of paper fluttered to the floor. He bent to pick it up. Looking up, he smiled at Sneha. It came easily.

'Raka has learnt to write beautifully!'

'I don't know what to say. As soon as she knew you were coming, she wanted to go away,' said Sneha.

Alam didn't reply.

'I've asked Raka's father to buy *ilish* tomorrow. I'll cook it for you.'

Alam smiled. 'Yes, Ganga's *ilish*. I haven't had it in a long time.'

Sneha was at the door, then she turned and asked, 'Shall I switch off the light?'

'Don't worry. I'll do it.'

'You can still come over, when you get the chance to – for us the road is closed forever. I was born there, grew up there – how that land haunts me, and your Meshomashai . . . . Almost ten years have passed – we have everything now – yet we feel like refugees!'

Silence began where words ended. The night lengthened. Alam picked up his watch and saw it was well past midnight. The noise of a solitary car broke the quiet of the night. A rickshaw went by, its bell ringing softly. Alam let go of his breath and went and sat on the bed.

Now he knew what to do. Continuity did manifest itself in blood, after all. Many years ago, before he left this house, Baba had offered his prayers on the terrace – Alam was witness to that. There he knelt, even though he had lost everything. But Alam didn't have that kind of faith. In the night, he could only wipe the teardrop gathering in the corner of his eye.

Picking up his suitcase, Alam murmured, 'You're honest too, Raka.'

SECTION TWO
ALIENATION

Pressure Cooker
Anjana Basu

Arushi was always a little afraid of the pressure cooker. It sat on top of the gas simmering like a shining bomb. 'Three whistles,' she had been told, 'otherwise the pressure builds up and it explodes.' The *bawarchi* had told her a whole host of cautionary tales about the daal splattering on the ceiling and windows smashed by the violence. 'Ghosh *memsahib* was lucky she was not blinded, the lid shot past her cheek…'

While he told her those stories, Ram went about the business of carefully browning the onions and the masala pastes, stirring them around noisily and cheerfully as if what he was saying was nothing at all. Then, he would fit the gasket followed by the lid and leave the thing to simmer while he went around the kitchen doing his other chores—as if nothing had happened at all. And then, hours later, or perhaps it was just 30 minutes, the hisses would begin to fill the apartment one after another.

Despite all Ram's training, Arushi never got the hang of it. Her mother was better at it, on the days she interested herself in such things—but Arushi's mother's interest gradually faded out of both their lives while Ram grew older and finally retired to his village. His sons preferred to run *paan* shops or become plumbers rather than go into cooking for a family like their father, so that was that. Arushi began to wrestle with the pressure cooker while her mother hired maid after maid and the cooking gradually slid into standard territory. Their family had always been known for the excellence of their lunches and dinners, and the decline upset Arushi. But, her mother continued as she always had—unruffled, yelling at the maids with no lessening of her volume. The number of maids fluctuated. In some months there were more and some months there were less.

Arushi was getting used to wiping the bathroom and folding the mosquito net. It was a practical way of looking at life, she thought, a way that her parents' generation would never understand, even though there were times when she wondered how things could have changed so much. Her father occasionally expostulated gently with her mother over the maids, but otherwise stayed quietly folded behind his newspaper on the verandah. Her mother joined him there in the afternoons when the maids had been dispatched to their ironing and cooking. The couple usually sat there long after the sun was gone and darkness fell, both their souls stranded in the wicker armchairs. When Arushi couldn't bear it any more, she would walk in, abruptly switch on the light and walk out again. But they sat silently as if the sudden illumination was some kind of aberration to be ignored.

She thought her parents' silence was a simmering kind of thing counterpointed by her mother's explosions. Arushi's lover—a man who had been cheating on his marriage for over ten years, and who had still not been able to leave his guilt behind—visited her cautiously and asked equally cautiously how they were and faded away again, leaving her with only the bruises on her collarbones for warmth.

It was a compromise she told herself. Without compromise, she would have exploded like Ram's pressure cooker stories a long ago. But, what could she say about a man who had married the wrong woman and then realising that—shackled himself with guilt except that she had loved him and refused to find someone else and pass the guilt on? So she stayed single, shackled by duty and guilt—with a day job that gave her some distraction from the kitchen and the clogged drain.

Not that the drain was clogged in the beginning and

certainly the maids would have dealt with it if she had let them. The clogging started after her father came home from the nursing home and a hush fell over her mother's ravings at the maids. The first few days of silence went overlooked, since Arushi was busy sending for medicines and organising bedpans. Her mother prowled around the house with the maids bringing sheets and cups of soup.

After a week, the hush was like a lid on the flat, echoing too loudly to be ignored. Her father feebly demanded to know what was wrong from his bed, but he got no answer. Arushi—caught between her work, her father and the last maid—stopped for breath and realised that something was certainly wrong.

You could have called it love, though Arushi was not sure that was what it was. Love was her standing all alone while her parents sneered at her lack of ability to find a man. Arushi had tolerated many things in the name of love, including a man so confused that he did not understand why she got under his skin until he had married the wrong woman. You could call what she was doing love, the cleaning of drains because she was doomed to run her parents' home instead of her own, rimming the soggy carrots and peas out from where her mother had rammed them. In the middle of the silence, her mother had stopped eating, or rather stopped clearing her plate in the meals that she and Arushi endured together. Those meals were counted in tablets, little blue pills that the doctor recommended after Arushi and her aunt had rushed her mother to a psychiatrist, leaving her father in the care of a handy cousin. 'Depression,' the psychiatrist had said gravely.

Relatives were understanding, it happened to everyone they murmured. And for a few weeks, there was a steady stream of aunts and cousins armed with stories and comfort food. But then the stream began to dry up in the face of her mother's refusal to communicate beyond a '*hoonh*' or a '*haanh*'. Everyone was sympathetic but no one had anything more to say. Gradually, Arushi's house shrank to the size of her mother's silence. Her lover said, 'Well, it is romantic…' and she found herself unable to correct him, especially since there were so many silences between them that could never be broken. He was a tall man who unfolded his long legs and folded them again in a way that always made her laugh, 'You're like a folding umbrella,' she told him.

'Well,' he said, kissing her, 'I'm folding myself up and going to buy something for my daughter's tiffin.' And he left her sitting there in the shadows—wondering whether it could be called love, after all.

Love could not be this greyness, this shambling walk and this dead silence. She found herself screaming at the remains on the plate but her mother ignored her as if she had said nothing at all, leaving the table in the shabby pink kaftan that she wore day after day now, in place of her crisp starched white saris.

It was chickpeas in the drain this time—the ones that had been simmered in the pressure cooker. Arushi found a spoon and scraped them out as best as she could. Perhaps, she thought, midnight would strike and she could turn into a chickpea. Nothing happened—the water dribbled warm over her hand, blood warm. Thoughts of blood dribbled through her head and she shook them away before taking herself and her wet hand to sleep.

Over the next few days, her father was better and soon able to sit on the verandah. He went back to slipping into darkness in the evening with Arushi's mother by his side. Arushi interviewed new maids and waited for the silence to disperse. Each maid she spoke to, seemed worse than the last. It was almost like the way their biscuit tins had turned from Wedgwood printed tins to plastic screw top bottles. She had one question that she asked all the maids, 'Can you handle a pressure cooker?' Her mother had never taught her how to interview maids, but she thought that would sort out the serious ones from the fly by nights. It seemed to work. She hired a girl who could handle the pressure cooker, chop and make chapattis.

The girl came to ask for orders the first morning dressed in a salwar kameez and stood there in front of Arushi's parents. Her mother's glaze flickered over the salwar kameez halted for a heartbeat and travelled on into indifference. Her mother had always hated maids dressed in salwar kameezes. They had floated in front of her eyes like a red rag and one of the maids had been sacked for a week of salwar kameezes. Her father's eyes had followed the salwar kameez and Arushi knew he was thinking the same thing. Her mother slumped in the chair again, a blotchy pink sack.

The psychiatrist had said that now Arushi's father was better, it would simply go away, but Arushi could see no signs of that. She wondered what the maids thought, or whether they ever thought at all while they ploughed through the housework with their minds on denim capris and boyfriends.

For days her mother went without washing her hair and the faded pink caftan that she wore had yellow streaks trailing down to the hem. Arushi wondered whether she would become like that in her old age and, if she did, who would even care? Her lover? He would probably succumb to another of his fit of guilt as he worried about his duty to the woman whose name he never brought to his lips.

Those yellow streaks made her shudder and think of pottery turning to plastic, Ram turning to part time domestics with awkward hands. Her mother had dragged combs through Arushi's hair when she was a child yanking it out almost by the roots as she tried to tame its springiness while the tears of pain trickled down Arushi's cheeks.

She had gone to school in tears too often to count,

but her hair had never surrendered. That mother who had stood for hours in front of the mirror teasing out her hair with a can of hair spray, so that she could go to a cocktail party with a neat beehive dome over her skull, now stood in those yellow streaks and the hair that stayed unwashed for weeks on end until Arushi fretted about lice. There had to be some kind of horrible logic to it.

The maids had to soak that caftan in neem wash to disinfect it and one or two of them refused. Arushi found herself sympathising with them, even as she argued about what the salaries were being paid for. Her mother floated through unaware of those yellow streaks or anything at all.

'You don't understand,' her father told her as he paced up and down like a grey ghost through the flat in what he thought was exercise, 'she can't help it!'

She did not understand, she had never understood.

The tomato and capsicum turning into brown gravy and then the whole thing capped with the heavy lid. She fumbled while doing it, almost dropping the whole thing on the floor. Theirs was an old pressure cooker, the heavy kind, not one of those sculpted bright red things that could be wrestled on and off easily. The maid made a face once she had it on, but Arushi ignored that, capping it with the whistle.

A noise startled her and she turned around to see her mother standing at the kitchen door staring blank faced. Arushi's fingers fumbled on the whistle but she kept hold of it and fitted it on its groove. Then she turned, took her mother by the arm and marched her to the verandah. The crook of that arm felt nothing at all, like something she could crush with one clench of her palm. Her fingers twitched but she controlled them. What she could not control was the hard hand that pulled her mother down the corridor and sent her towards the chair with a harder push than she need have. Her mother stumbled, hovered for a moment in mid-air, then hit the chair, legs splayed and glared her as she sat.

Three whistles spaced out, like sudden explosions through the flat.

The Hunter
Soumitro Das

Wolves.

I can hear them baying all around me.

We were in the jungle. There were five of us.

The wolves numbered a little over 200.

Now, there are fifteen of them left.

But I am alone.

My companions have all been swallowed up—swallowed up by the night with its glittering eyes and bared fangs.

I fight on.

We had been summoned by the King of Pygmies whose kingdom was being ravaged by wolf packs. They carried off men, women, children, poultry and cattle—leaving the countryside desolate and stricken. Two years ago, the King of the Pygmies had entrusted us, men of the north, with the mission of rooting out this plague from his domain. Our reputation as hunters was spread far and wide and there is no exaggeration when I say that three of our musketeers have sent an entire herd of elephants to elephant-heaven.

The King provided us with more than adequate cottages, provisions, arms and ammunition in the jungle and asked his priests to sacrifice 56 bulls to the gods.

We began our hunt at the beginning of the hot season when the wolves had to move far and wide in search of water. That was also the season of their depredation. We built a stockade around our cottages and took turns to keep watch at night. Three of us would go out to the jungle villages to protect the people from the wolves.

We spent long hours in the night, smoking and chatting, until we heard the first pitter-patter of hooves, the first low howl, the rustling of vegetation and then the stillness familiar to all hunters—the stillness of predators watching you. Instead of pouring through a single point, as it were, the pack would divide itself into groups of 40 each and attack us from all directions at the same time. We were hard pressed to keep our flanks covered.

We herded the population onto a piece of land and lit fires all around them, so that we could tackle the pack in the clear. Moonlit nights were the best, we could kill up to a dozen at a time. The rest of the time, we held torches in our left hand while we maneuvered our guns with our right.

Gradually, they grew to recognise us and our ways. and they held consultations among themselves. They began sending out patrols, so we wouldn't know which village would be attacked next.

We decided to take the fight to them, to their own territory—to the jungle.

We had a hard time, especially when five or six wolves would leap at us at the same time. That is when the injuries began and some of us were incapacitated for short spells. It took us many months of hard hunting in the darkness of the jungle, to subjugate the packs, one by one, until diminished in numbers, they grew wary of us. We grew aware that their thoughts were turning less and less towards their prey and more and more toward us.

They no longer went to the villages. We didn't know what they ate, but we shot at some gnawing at the roots, gobbling up snakes, rats and birds in broad daylight.

At night, they hunted, just like us.

They took four of my companions, one after the other, waiting for the moment when we would lose sight of each other—or on the way back to the stockade, or in a ferocious ambush that would take us unawares.

My companions are gone.

But I have no time to mourn for them.

I have been alone in the stockade for the last six months, surrounded by the remnants of the packs—

about fifteen of them, famished, unwashed, hallucinating, worn out, unable to give up their hatred of me and go hunt down some prey instead.

My provisions are running out and I am desperately short of ammunition as well.

The King of the Pygmies has forgotten about me. His kingdom is free of the wolf menace.

They hang around me all the time now…

And I am not, how shall I put it…I am not well.

Strange things have happened lately.

They began soon after my last companion was devoured in front of me by six wolves, just outside the stockade.

This last act of savagery seems to have sapped all their energy.

Now they spend their time circling around the stockade—listless, heads bent low, baying a little now and then, but strangest of all, looking at me timidly, whenever I take my occasional pot shot, as if begging for my forgiveness.

Or else, they gather in front of the stockade gate, take in the sun—looking weary and disinterested.

They have become vegetarians like cattle. I see them grazing on grass, on leaves, blinking myopically at each other, ruminating, their memories effaced by two years of decimation.

I don't know what to make of this strange behavior.

At last, one of them whistles across to me one afternoon, as I sit smoking my pipe in my verandah.

We want to talk, he says.

About what? I ask.

About this situation, says the wolf.

All right, I said, send your representative and don't get too close.

I cock my musket at them, finger on trigger.

The leader of the pack ambles up to me, bends his head at an obsequious angle and has what I thought was a sly expression on his face, which on a wolf, looks uncouth.

Make it snappy, I say.

He looks hither and thither as if unwilling to come to the point.

You are on your own now, he says, coughing a little. He looks ill.

So what? I say.

How are you going to get back to where you came from? says the wolf.

That's none of your business, I say.

Yes, maybe, he says, but we know you are short on food and your ammunition is running out too.

I held up my musket and pulled the safety latch back.

When he heard the click, he retreated a few steps.

Don't shoot, he says.

I take a shot at his legs. He manages to dodge the

bullet and scamper back to the rest of the pack waiting for him at a distance.

I am overcome with exhaustion, sleeplessness and hunger.

Nothing happens over the next few days.

I wake up one morning to find that the fire has gone out and the leader of the pack sitting in the yard, in front of my cottage. He was alone. I had no idea how he had managed to sneak in.

I reach for my musket and take aim.

He gets up and takes to his feet, leaping over the fence as best as he can, with his skinny legs.

Why didn't he attack me? I said to myself.

I go back to my routine—checking the ammunition, the provisions, keeping an eye out for trouble, listening to the hooves circling and recircling the stockade in search of God knows what.

A few weeks later, I find the carcass of a deer calf at my doorstep.

I don't understand where it has come from and what it is supposed to mean.

I look out east from the stockade and I see the pack gathered there, slowly swishing their tails, not looking at me, just hanging around.

It's a little gift for you, says the leader of the pack, with a smirk on his face, bending his head low.

I am thunderstruck.

I take the carcass and throw it back at them.

I don't want any more gifts from you, you scoundrels, I shout at them angrily, firing a single shot in the air to disperse them.

But they refused to go away.

Then I shoot one of them.

The wolves run away, but not for very long. They are soon back on the prowl.

They no longer look as threatening, but they irritate me with their inane laughter, their coughs and snorts and the forlorn, tranquil expressions on their faces.

They recommence showering me with what I suppose they would call 'gifts' odds and ends picked up from here and there, guavas, a parakeet, sometimes a fish, mushrooms and strange tubers they had discovered all by themselves.

I hurl everything back at them until my arms hurt from saying no. My supplies continue to dwindle and there is no news from the King of the Pygmies, whom I am dependent on to find my way back.

Go away, I shouted at the pack, and in my rage, waste half a dozen bullets on them.

They stand at a safe distance and laugh at me.

Don't be scared, the leader says. We won't harm you.

The pack laughs

Go away! I shout once again.

A hunter never asks his prey to go away, he hunts

him. These creatures are no longer wolves. They are now giggling and jumping around, devoid of all dignity, like a bunch of immature macacas.

But they know I am alone and possibly helpless.

No longer able to attack me as before—having abandoned their carnivorous ways for good—they were content to irritate and harass me. They continue to deposit 'gifts' in front of my cottage as frequently as I throw them back at them.

I myself have grown so feeble that I can no longer perform my daily chores. My hands have begun to tremble. I take care to keep my musket loaded, if only as a reminder of who I once was and what had been my mission in this country.

About a month ago, the hunger began.

I have about two weeks of supplies remaining.

Every morning I stare at the nourishment lying there in front of me in the yard like an insult addressed to my growing solitude and physical disability. It is like a Trojan horse for the spirit.

Shall I eat it?

Hunger gnaws at my stomach. I lick my lips, take sips of water from my canteen.

As my condition deteriorates, the quality of the 'offerings' declines. The wolves have probably understood that they are dealing with a dying man who will sell his soul cheap when the time comes.

It happened the day before yesterday.

In the evening, when all was dark and no one was looking, not even the wolves who had lost their brilliant eyesight, I crawled out to the yard and grabbed the rotten fruit the wolves had left for me in the morning, which I hadn't had the strength to hurl back at them. I wolfed it down.

I was immediately struck with remorse and shame. I decided to strengthen my resolve not to permit these lapses to occur in the future.

But every morning, I found that the Hunger had grown and I would pounce on everything the wolves had brought for me. I was devouring my own instincts.

I stopped cleaning and loading my musket which had grown rusty and perfectly useless.

The wolves too, had lost their fangs.

They giggled when they saw me eating the food they had left for me. In the jungle, they were the only society I had.

They tried to bay occasionally, but it sounded more like the bleating of lambs.

This was no consolation for me.

Every night, as I lay on my bed, weak and feverish, I dreamed of the north, of its hilly landscapes and crystal clear lakes. I thought of my abject surrender and wept.

I could not even pray, for I had forgotten the names of my gods and the manner of calling after them.

Gradually, the wolves crept into the stockade and took up permanent abode there. They lazed around in the sun, with their cubs, giggled and coughed and cracked jokes and took fear at the slightest noise.

I no longer had the strength to chase them away.

Then one day, the leader of the pack came over to me and said, You are lonely.

I was lying in a corner, unshaven for weeks, unwashed, hungry, in tatters, unable to employ my mind for anything but the thought of food.

Look at yourself, said the wolf leader. You are a real sight. You can't even feed yourself anymore.

He spat this out from the corner of his mouth.

It is we, he continued, who bring you food. And yet, you lie in your corner, ignoring us, disdaining our company.

He looked at me malevolently.

Who do you think you are? he said. Some kind of a big game hunter? An ace marksman? A thing that walks on two legs? Let me see you walk now! Go on, show us, how you walk!

A spirit moved inside me when I heard these words. I tried getting up from my bed, but I couldn't. I rolled over on my stomach, heaved myself up on all fours and crawled a few paces into the courtyard.

The wolves roared with laughter.

The leader of the pack came up to me and said, You

see, now, you are one of us.

He had a mocking expression on his face.

Listen, he said, as if speaking to a child. Be reasonable. You can't go back anymore and the Pygmies have forgotten about you.

It was like listening to my own vomit.

Let us forget our past quarrels, said the leader, gently. Let us bury the hatchet and let us live in peace and harmony.

What are you suggesting? I barked back at him, for my voice had suddenly grown coarse and gruff, almost like a growl, the hair on my body had multiplied and now formed a furry coat and my tongue had grown longer and thicker.

Why don't you join the pack? said the leader. That way you can hunt for food like the rest of us. After all, it is better to be an honorable wolf than to be a thing that crawls on all fours. You could even lead the pack. You are bigger than the rest of us here and with a proper diet, you can be the strongest too, so why not? Plus there are some nice females in the pack who are…well…how shall I put it?…who…er…want to breed with you, how about it?

And then, he looked up at me and what he saw frightened him out of his wits.

He tried to flee but it was too late.

I pounced upon him and sliced off his neck with my fangs, savoring the taste and smell of blood on my lips.

I ate him, morsel by morsel, until my former strength returned to me.

But I was still hungry. The pack had disappeared.

There was a Pygmy village nearby. I decided to make my way there to see if I could find some food, a lamb, a piece of poultry or a human.

The moon had risen.

I lifted up my snout and bayed.

The Firebird
Saikat Majumdar

The Party he knew. Who didn't? Their office stood right next to the football grounds, under the bright paintings of the hammer, sickle and the star. The men played football all afternoon and then gathered in the room in the evening to paint banners for strikes and protest marches. Grim older men in shirts and pyjamas broke up fights on the football fields and brawls in the government ration shops. Everybody knew it was much

---

An excerpt from *Firebird* (Hachette India, 2015) by Saikat Majumdar. It explores the relationship of conservative Bengali society with the different cultures of theatre in post-independence Calcutta. It reflects on a young boy's obsessive relation with his mother's life as a theatre actress and his coming of age in the backdrop of political bullies, actors, and other figures from the world of performance and politics.

easier to settle disputes at the Party office than at the local police station. They both belonged to the Party but the police were lazy and would not work without bribes. Things moved fast at the Party office and the cadres always helped people in trouble.

But Ori had never heard of the citizen's council. Who were they?

'What would you like to eat?' Abir placed a menu before him, a long sheet of laminated paper, smudged near the corners. A tall glass appeared before him, the fizz settling slowly on the dark pool of Coca Cola in it. Through the blue haze of cigarette smoke dancing around the table, the glass looked like a dream. He hesitated.

'I want to go home,' suddenly he felt uneasy.

It made them unhappy. Anxiety clouded the table. 'Why?' Abir reached out and held his hand. 'Come on. I know you love Chinese.'

'Relax, Oritro,' Trinankur's voice caressed him. 'What would you like to eat?' Across the dimness the councillor's eyes were aimed at him, straight, kind and soft.

'But,' Ori said. 'I have to go home. They will worry.'

'Who will?' Abir asked his brows dancing.

Ori fell silent, not knowing what to say.

'Let's order some starters,' Trinankur said with a smile. 'What would you like?'

It was kindness you could not spurn. Kindness that caressed him slowly. 'Fried prawns!' he said.

'Good choice.' The smoke-drowned owner of the beauty parlour spoke for the first time.

'And what else?' Abir asked.

More! Hesitantly, Ori looked through the menu. Szechwan noodles with gravy?

More food was ordered around the table, endless names ticked off on the menu. Dreamily, Ori stared at the picture at the top of the menu – a skinny old Chinese man with a thin, pointy beard. In a chef's uniform, face split open in a cartoon grin, prancing along with a whole roast chicken balanced on a tray.

'Funny picture,' he heard himself say, quite before he realized he had. The sound of his own voice made him anxious; he stopped short.

'Oh yeah,' Abir leaned in to take a look and then drew back. An undercurrent of laughter trembled around the table.

'Do you still draw, Oritro? Trinankur asked. There was a softness in his eyes, a softness brushed with a smile. It made Ori eager to talk, but all he could do was nod.

'I remember the Vishnu you painted in the children's sit-and-draw contest,' Trinankur said, his eyes gazing off towards the swinging door to the kitchen, squeaking close and open every other second.

'Year before last right? It was beautiful.'

Ori looked up and stared at Trinankur.

'He had it down to the last detail,' Trinankur looked

around the table, a glow on his face. 'The chakra, the lotus, everything. And he was probably just eight at the time.'

Trinankur remembered it clearly.

It created a warm feeling in Ori's chest.

'I remember it from the awards ceremony that year.' It was as if Trinankur knew what Ori was thinking. I was struck by the choice. And then the details. The details.' He repeated.

A hand came to rest on Ori's shoulders. Softly. Abir's.

'Hey, you don't like Coca Cola?' His voice was warm and soft. "You haven't touched it. '

Ori sipped at the Coca-Cola. The sweet fizz simmered on his tongue and made him faintly nauseated. Large plates of noodles and entrees arrived at the table. Gold-fried balls of prawns, chicken and capsicum in thick, fire-like sauce, cubes of what looked like boneless fish in heaps of sautéed onions and chili, more plates of dense and dark sauce with tiny islands of food sticking their heads out. As the waiters started ladling out the food on the large china plates laid out before them, a fractured chorus went around the table, directing the fried prawns on Ori's plate. And a good helping of Szechwan noodles. And some chilli chicken. And that he should eat more.

Undecided, Ori took another sip at his Coca-Cola. It did taste bitter with a bizarre twist to it sharpened by the swirling cigarette smoke all around him.

'Try the fish too,' Abir ladled a large portion onto his plate. 'It's pan-fried.' He used the serving spoon to make space on Ori's plate, separating the noodles and the prawns in neat, distinct zones with a tenderness that saddened Ori for reasons he couldn't grasp.

'Why did you choose to draw a picture of Vishnu?' Trinankur asked in a voice touched with wonder.

'I like to copy things,' Ori said. 'I copied it from my mind.'

'Where did you see it?'

'My Mummum has a framed photo of Vishnu in her prayer room. She prays before it every evening. It's a really nice picture.'

'His grandmother,' Abir said, pushing the tall glass of Coca-Cola closer to Ori.

The fried prawn had made Ori thirsty. He took a long swig at the Coca-Cola. The nauseating fizz went down his throat like a flood of cold vomit. His head swam as if he was afloat in air.

'Your Mummum is your favourite person in the house, isn't she?' Trinanukur asked, his voice soft. Ori nodded quietly. It was not something he could describe. His Mummum was the source of everything that was reassuring and real. But he liked to hide from the world. He couldn't imagine a life without Mummum and yet he was desperate to grow out of this sticky, shameful need.

Trinankur was silent now, but his eyes remained

locked with Ori's. In a kind of a pact that excluded the others at the table, there was safety in Trinankur's company, in his gentle smile. Ori looked down again, at the crescent of prawns across his plate.

'You tell her everything, don't you?' It was strange listening to Dushtu's voice. It kept growing fainter. It seemed to come from far away.

'So tell us,' he leaned forward. 'When did you first see your mother with Samiran Uncle?'

Terror clutched his heart like a black sharp-clawed bat, killing his desire for sweet-and-sour fish. An acid wave of vomit rose to his throat. All eyes were on him now, even those that pretended to look away. Trinankur just sat there chewing his food furiously, his pimples jumped up and down as his jaws moved.

'We know you've seen them at his house,' Tatai's voice crawled towards him, like a buried animal slowly coming back to life. 'Doing things to each other.'

'Oritro?' The voice cut through the darkness. 'How many times have you seen your mother with Samiran?'

His mother?

The woman who'd fought with vultures. Over her brother's grave. The one who'd been Antigone out in the windy nakedness of the Maidan grounds under the dark evening sky? The stubborn, hot-headed woman who pierced through her clothing of shyness to silently fight everybody around her?

He wanted to eat. The fragrance of fried prawns had merely sharpened his appetite. He tried to ladle some sauce with his spoon, stab at a piece of meat with his fork. But his hands, weak blobs of jelly, couldn't make sense of the darkness on his plate. It was frustrating and strangely it made him want to laugh. The laughter weighed down on him, wrestling him to the ground, pinning his arms at the elbows till the fork clattered against the rim of his plate and bounced on to the table. 'You're not doing this right,' Trinankur's voice came from the wilderness. 'I was getting to it gently.'

'He's a child, remember?'

'Yes, I saw that,' a voice whirled. 'Going on and on about paintings, then it would be school, and if he liked Mughlai food better than Chinese. And then, cricket. Smooth!'

'You need patience for some things. I didn't win the elections three times running being a brute.'

'Who do you think you're doing a favour?' It was moving, the intense energy in Tatai's voice. Quickly, he tunred to Ori again. 'Does your mother go to this man's home often? Do they meet elsewhere?'

'There's no one else in the graveyard,' Ori heard his own voice come from a distance. 'Just the vultures.'

'What?' Dushtu looked like he had been punched in the face.

The cutting had been from the leading Bengali daily.

You had to squint to see the caption beneath the picture. Garima Basu in the role of Antigone. Produced by Max Mueller Bhavan.

'The vultures were live.' The words circled around his head again and again, before he could utter them. 'And the Germans taught her to jump across the trenches. She had her brother's dead body across her shoulders.'

Trinankur reached across the table, held Ori's hand. He leaned in closer. Electrified, he pulled back. His pimples swelled like red dots on his cheeks as anger flushed his face. 'Did you give him booze?' He looked around the table, ready to kill.

Abir moved the glass of Coca-Cola away from Ori. But not fast enough for Trinankur, who snatched it away, the dark liquid sloshing around inside. He sniffed at it, thumped it down hard on the table.

'This is rum laced with Coke,' Trinankur thundered. 'Whose idea was it?'

'Was supposed to be Coke laced with rum,' Abir said. 'I guess someone got carried away.'

'The vultures were perched on the wall across the graveyard,' Ori said. 'Not stuffed birds. Live ones.'

They didn't seem to care anymore.

'This was a mistake,' Trinankur said, despair in his voice. 'The whole thing.'

'Get real, Dada,' Dushtu said. 'The citizen's council has sorted out a lot of messed-up families, and sometimes you need to twist the knife a bit. Nothing the Party doesn't know already.'

'This is a family we care about. They've lived here for generations,' Trinankur's voice boomed. 'This is not some drunken rickshawallah who beats up his woman in the slums every day. You can't just throw a kid like him in a pool of rum and get the scoop out of him.'

Right next to Trinankur, Tatai roused himself from a sleepy darkness. When had he taken Abir's place? And why was Abir nowhere to be seen?

A clammy hand wound around Ori's back, rested heavily on his right shoulder. 'You saw them in bed? How… er… you remember what they had on?' Stubby fingers slipped past the collar of Ori's T-shirt and rubbed his skin gently, ever so gently, to the rhythm of the questions, repeated in a whisper. 'Or did they?'

He was a smooth man. His hand a bloc of kindness on Ori's skin, he looked across the table to Trinankur, 'Do you realize how serious a problem this is for us? At least five families have told us that with their own daughters growing up here. This woman is a shame to have around in the para. She spends all her evenings in the theatre halls in dirty neighbourhoods and comes home way past midnight. Rupa boudi came to my house last Friday and told me that the woman sleeps with other men right in front of the boy. He told his grandmother everything just the previous night.'

'In the end, it is the Party who has to watch out for the para,' the grating voice shot through the air again. 'I told Rupa boudhi, don't say a word. We'll find out what happened. And then we'll fix her.'

The first bout of vomit rocked Ori from within before spurting out of his mouth. Stunned, Tatai recoiled. Watery, with tiny islands of food floating in them, the vomit streamed into the fire-red gravy of the sweet-and-sour fish, flooding the boat-like bowl in which he had been served, spilling on the table. The second wave shot spasms through his small body, his head dropping down into the bowl of sweet-and-sour fish, sweet-and-sour vomit.

Tatai's right arm wrapped around him again, this time, clutching his ribs. It was a deep hug that squeezed more vomit out of his quaking frame, the acid burning his nose. 'Should have gone easy on the booze,' he said, softly massaging the shaking body. 'Need to take him home now.'

Chairs screeched against the floor. Foggy outlines of bodies rose together; more hands hugged him and helped him to his feet. His hair was now soaked with sweat. He felt the dampness settle into his skull.

The Watch Without Hands
Shoma A Chatterji

Seema received a small package in the post. It was from her maternal grandfather who had passed away a fortnight ago. They could not attend the funeral and other rites because her mother was not keeping well. Taking a train to Igatpuri would have been too much of a strain for her. True, that Igatpuri was just a few miles away and the train ride from Dadar to Igatpuri would have taken only a few hours. But her mother was not in a position to travel and Seema lacked the courage to leave her alone in the care of old Meera Tai. Meera Tai was probably older than her mother and was arthritic. Slightly bent at the waist, her walk was crooked. Work-wise, she kept up her standards. Her *puran polis* stuffed with gram dal paste and jaggery were delicious. Her *besan laddus* were soft and greasy because she always fried the gram flour in pure ghee and stuffed every *laddu* with raisins and cashew nuts that you could feel at first bite. These days, she was forever muttering to herself. Seema and her mother had gotten used to her muttering. They could not imagine life without Meera Tai. She kept the house spic and span and also cooked for the three of them.

Seema's maternal uncle had called to inform them that her grandfather had kept a small gift for her and he would dispatch it soon. Seema had no feelings at all. She had been detached from her mother's family for a long time. She was indifferent to what her grandfather had laid aside for her and when she would get it. When she felt the square package in her hands, she felt no emotion. She walked back to her room to keep the box on the built-in concrete shelf on the wall and forgot all about it.

She worked in the electric supply office as an upper division clerk. Her job was spiced with gossip and it helped her keep her mind away from worrying about her mother and her medication, Meera Tai's aches and pains—Till the day ended and she had to take the shared rickshaw back home.

That evening, Seema remembered the little box. After a cup of tea and her favourite biscuits, she took the box from the shelf and sat on her bed, ready to open it. Before she could unwrap the paper packaging, her mother called her from the other room and she left the box and walked to her mother.

'What packet did the courier boy bring this morning?' she asked and Seema was surprised that she had noticed.

'I haven't opened it yet. It is from *Bara Mama* in Igatpuri,' said Seema. Her mother's face lit up in a soft smile. Seema was surprised because she had no clue that her mother was attached to her parental family because she neither expressed it in any way nor showed any desire to visit them at Igatpuri. This rift, if one could call it that, did not have any back story of family feuds around cross marriages or property divisions. It faded away, fallen apart, bit by little bit, like the petals of a dried up flower, or shards of a broken mirror, slowly and surely, till only some shreds of memories remained. Or did they? Were there memories left to be mulled over? Her mother's 'family' faded away from their radar because time did not allow them to keep in touch or rather, the people concerned were not really bothered. She hardly remembered how many times they visited Igatpuri for any family function. They were invited, but they also knew that they would gracefully decline and stay away. Seema had no clue why they did not go to Igatpuri or why her uncles and aunts did not visit them and no one asked them.

Both her parents were such social recluses that they did not interact with anyone—relatives, extended family members, neighbours, even colleagues. Seema had imbibed a bit of that wilful alienation from social links so her mother's smile was surprising.

'Go see what's in it. I want to know,' her mother said and gave her a small push towards her room. 'I was just about to open it when you called,' said Seema as she walked back. But her mother forgot to ask her what it contained later on, like always and this time, Seema was happy about her forgetfulness.

The unwrapping of the paper packaging was a process of discovery and intrigue. At least, she knew who had sent it because the name and address of the sender was written in black ink on one side of the package. It was probably her cousin's name—her elder uncle's son who she had met only once as a child—she could not recall his name anymore. 'Igatpuri' at the end of the address convinced her that it had come from her uncle.

There are packages where even the sender remains a mystery. Seema used her slender, long fingers slowly so that the wrapper did not tear off somewhere. By habit, she was disciplined and meticulous. She tried to open it carefully. Finally, a small red box, like the small ring boxes you get in jewellery shops, made its appearance. She opened it gingerly, with the curiosity of a little child and found a man's wrist watch lodged inside with a metallic band around it. The dial had the numbers printed on it but no hands.

Seema was scared. She felt a sense of *déjà vu* wash over her softly, like water flowing down her back under a shower. Where and when had she experienced this feeling before? She had never seen a watch with no hands on the dial and only numbers. The watch was a tiny, inanimate object that had no life of its own and began to acquire life only when someone strapped it on one's wrist. Why the fear? A watch, a table clock, wall clock or a grandfather clock always had big hands to depict the hour, the minute and the second hand. She never imagined that a watch could exist without hands. She carefully turned the watch around in her palm, trying to examine it closely but could not detect anything to indicate the lack of the hands. She would not have understood if there was any technical fault. What did she know about watches or clocks?

Seema placed the watch carefully back into the box, slipping it into the wedge in the box so that it did not slip to this side or that. She closed the box and placed it back on the open shelf. She found her hands shaking a little. She had no idea why. By nature, she was not a nervous person. She was a single, independent, working woman who had never married and now she did not believe that she would ever marry. She was nervous about creating a relationship that would trap her independence. She was once in love with a distant cousin, Rahul, who had lived with them for a year while studying engineering at the IIT. It seemed he too returned her feelings and they had a brief romance for a year or so. 'Romance' was confined to a few secret hugs and kisses. The secrecy was more exciting than the act, she realised. They had indulged in sex too, once, but Seema did not enjoy it at all because she was a virgin and she had bled badly and found the experience quite painful.

Rahul had a wrist watch with a radium dial that lit up in the dark. Sometimes, you could not see the minute hand if the light fell at a certain angle. He would point this out to Seema. But Seema was scared. Any watch minus a hand, or two hands, scared her for something she had no idea about. She would request Rahul to take off his watch when he came home. Rahul would look back at her with a curious smile but take off the watch. Then one day, he misplaced the watch in the local train and was very unhappy. It was a birthday gift from his father. But Seema secretly felt very happy.

The lost watch haunted her for days. She would dream of hundreds of wrist watches with one hand or both hands missing—chasing her on an open street. These watches had dials with numbers but no hands or sometimes, only one hand that kept moving around the circumference of the dial which scared her for no reason she could put a finger on. She would wake up in a cold sweat, gulp down glasses of water and go back to sleep. She did not share this with her parents because 'sharing' of confidences was not a part of the family pattern. In fact, the family did not have any 'pattern'. They would respond with blank faces and get back to what they were doing at that moment. Seema did not mind and did not share her fears with them.

What did a watch minus hands really mean? She had unconsciously made a habit of glancing at everyone's wrists on her way to work, while returning from work and at work. All those watches had three hands but she often felt some of them had no hands. She had this fixation with watches—with or without hands. She did not know why and did not even want to find out why.

Her affair with Rahul was short-lived. The boy was not serious about the affair. It worked for him so long as he lived in the city. He was entirely focussed on his studies. Once he went away, he never contacted her or her parents again. Seema found it strange. But this did not hurt her because looking back, she too, was not very serious about the short affair. She always felt that she was weak in the emotions department. She had inherited it from her parents. They were almost emotionless. Their behaviour and their way of life proved this through small realities. Her birthdays were never celebrated and even when in school, the teacher and the class sang 'Happy Birthday' together, she felt shy and more embarrassed than happy. Her parents did not have friends who visited them and nor did they visit them either. Her father never brought any office gossip home nor did they have much conversation around the dinner table. It was a peaceful environment and Seema had no complaints because she did not know any other kind of life. Meera Tai offered the only spark of relief in a rather boring world. But for Seema and her parents, life was anything but 'boring.' This was the life they were used to and they never felt the need to know about any other world that existed beyond the one they lived—day in and day out.

They saw TV but did not 'watch' it if that was the right distinction. Her father saw the news channels and her mother switched on to some soap. They did all this with their poker faced expressions glued to their stone-like faces while Seema sometimes sat with them. Mostly she did not because her interest lay in reading. Reading opened so many different worlds for her with every sentence, page and every chapter. Reading took her to different countries— into families she never knew before, introduced her to people she did not know existed and subconsciously, she learnt to share their travels, joys and sorrows.

She was a member at the local library and also bought books for herself. She had filled three built-in shelves of the open wall cabinet with her books which she did not mind reading repeatedly as her choice was random but carefully designed. Books were her friends, lovers, companions, and in a manner of speaking, an alternative, surreal world in which she could see the characters come to life. She felt she would be able to touch, feel and smell them if she stretched an arm. But she had a slight tremor in one hand and she stopped from stretching it lest it brought back her fear of that slight tremor. And without being conscious of it, she looked for the presence or absence of watches and clocks in every novel, short story and play she read. Was it because she had a tremor in her hand that stopped her from wearing a watch? It never occurred to her to find a medical solution to her problem because she did not consider it a medical problem at all. She thought of it as an embarrassment. In due course of time, she was convinced that this tremor was part of her personality and she did not wish to get cured! It was as simple as that! But she desperately longed to wear a watch. She had a watch that her father had presented her with but she did not wear it. It was not in her father's nature to comment even if he may have noticed it.

She had once seen a film in which the protagonist had been gifted a watch by his mother in which the dial had no hands. The old man, a retired professor, kept looking at that watch time and again. The film did not explain why—you were supposed to interpret the answer. She did not remember the name of the film but that memory of the old man looking at that watch never left her.

How did it really matter if a watch did not have hands? What did watch hands really do? They counted hours and minutes and seconds on your behalf. They determined the rules of your life. She had read *Watch Without Hands* long ago in which one of the main characters had blood cancer and had decided that a watch was a warning for death. Was it really? While in college, she had met a boy who refused to wear a wrist watch. When asked why, he laughed and said, 'I do not want a watch to imprison me in a cage of regulated time. I want to be free of any regimentation of my time. I want to control my time myself.' Some had laughed away not understanding what he meant while others looked puzzled or nodded their heads and walked away.

Seema was not bothered. For her, thinking was too strenuous an exercise—an exercise in futility. But the watch with the missing hands forced her to engage in this very strenuous exercise called "thinking." She had no idea why and when men began to trap time into boxes labelled with names like years, months, days, hours, minutes and seconds but they had done it all the same. They had invented the watch in different usable and varied versions. She felt that men did not realise that time is fluid, flawless and free-flowing. We have no control over it— no matter how much we try to box it and resist its control over our life—and more importantly—our death. Seema went to the shelf and took out the watch to take a look. Her left hand was shaking as usual. She strapped the watch around her shaky wrist and strutted about the room. She stood in front of the mirror and preened. She lifted her left wrist and looked at the watch strapped to it. She placed the hand on her waist and struck a pose and smiled at herself. She could tangibly feel her fear fade away like a lit candle melting down to a circle of wax.

The next morning, when Seema wore the watch, not bothered about the dial without hands before leaving for work, the door bell rang. She walked up to the door before Meera Tai could reach it with her painful limp. It was the same courier boy who had come the day before. With a rather apologetic smile, he asked for the packet adding that the packet he had delivered the day before was the wrong one. Seema looked at her wrist and noticed that the tremor had disappeared. She took it off her wrist, put it back in the box and handed it back to the boy. He took it back with a grateful smile and handed her a different package, that looked identical to the one she had just handed over but it did not have the wrapping.

'I am sorry that the wrapping is gone. I had delivered the wrong package to another customer yesterday and this one is yours,' said the boy. Seema took a look at the embroidered slogan on his red uniformed tee-shirt and cap. The slogan said, 'guaranteed delivery of the right package to the right customer' and smiled to herself. 'That package was also from Igatpuri to Andheri (West)' said the boy absent-mindedly, taking a look at his bag as he walked away.

That night, Seema had a strange dream. She dreamt of a large, green field where she was running to try and get a hold of two giant clock hands racing through the fields, one big and the other a bit smaller. But as she ran, they ran further away from her till slowly, they disappeared across the horizon. Then, she woke up in a cold sweat. She opened the package of the wrist watch that had arrived and found that the watch had the hour, minute and second hands intact. The hands winked back at her as if they had found their long-lost friend. Seema strapped it around her left wrist which had lost its tremor, rested her head on the bedstead and smiled. Whether a watch had the hour, minute and seconds hand or not did not bother her anymore. Her time was hers—fluid, flawless and free.

SECTION THREE
BELONGING

About Time, Jessica
Rimi B Chatterjee

Jessica snipped another millimetre off the little monster's fringe, stepped back and considered the brat's squashed and disapproving face in the mirror. 'That'll do,' snapped the little monster's mother, giving Jessica a glare. 'We don't want her looking like a *mem*, do we?'

Jessica said nothing. She unpeeled the white sheet from the little monster's body and let the hair clippings fall onto the floor. Jessica Flora Rosario was aware that she was a mem—a white woman—in name only. Her

---

An early, shorter version of *Jessica* appeared in *Vislumbres: Bridging India and Iberoamerica* 1 (2008).

skin was darker than the little monster and her mother put together. What was more, she had been born and brought up here, in Ganguly Bagan on the southern margins of Calcutta, one of the many children that had overrun the big crumbling house of Freddie Rosario three decades ago.

Most of those kids were gone now—Peter, counting change in a ticket window overseas in Australia; Roger, drunk and singing 'Lead Kindly Light' in the middle of the street till he was crushed under a bus; Susan and Mary, lost somewhere in the slums of Bombay with stars in their eyes; Florian, her twin brother with the easy smile, prowling the city in search of another fix; and Amelia, sweet little fourteen-year-old Amelia, child of Freddie's old age just before he kicked the bucket.

Amelia was lying in bed at home, counting the cracks on the ceiling and waiting for her big sister to bring home the day's earnings from the hairdressing saloon. She couldn't go to school—Amelia had very definite ideas of what she wanted to learn from the world, and the teachers complained too much. Jessica puffed talcum powder onto the big soft brush and dusted the little monster's neck. Fussing and clucking, her mother paid with bad grace and left. Jessica sagged onto a stool and kicked moodily at the clippings on the floor.

'Sweep those up,' snapped Rosy, her boss. Rosy's real name was Shuchorita, but everybody knew you couldn't get ahead in the hairdressing business if you didn't have an Anglo-Indian name. 'Rosy' in fact was stolen from 'Rosario' and soggily pronounced 'Rojy' by the entire neighbourhood. Jessica groaned and got the broom, swept the mess into a corner. Then she slumped in the chair that the little monster had vacated and gave Rosy an appealing look.

'Will you do my eyebrows for me, Rosy?'

'Hah! You good for nothing, get up from there. Customers will come in a minute and what'll they do when they see a fat black ding in a frock hogging their place?' Rosy said haughtily.

'I'm not a ding,' Jessica said sulkily. 'Don't call me an Anglo. I don't have a drop of English blood in my veins. My ancestors were Portuguese!'

'*Eeeesh*! If you're so Portuguese then, what are you doing working for Rojy in Ganguly Bagan?' And Rosy shouted with laughter and shambled off to light the burner under the hot wax.

Jessica stuck her tongue out so hard at Rosy's back that her mouth hurt for hours afterwards. When she got home she was in a foul mood. The day's takings barely paid for the groceries, and she needed new shoes. On top of that, Amelia whined all through dinner. 'Eat your doll!' Jessica snapped, pouring thick lentil soup over Amelia's rice. 'Your eyes are bigger than your stomach, what?' Jessica asked.

'Why can't we have steak? We're supposed to have steak,' whined Amelia.

'Steak! One tight slap you'll get, Amelia, how long are you going to be the baby of the family?'

Amelia pouted. 'Always.'

Jessica shook her head. 'I don't get it,' she said softly. 'What's the matter with us? There's you, with half a brain in your silly head. There's me, taking orders from a bleddy cow who calls me names and laughs. All the men are abroad, or boozards, or dead. Why do we stay on? Why can't we go...to Portugal? Isn't that where we came from? Amelia? Would you like to go to Portugal, men?'

'Can we have steak there?'

Jessica pondered this idea. 'I don't know. But I've heard everything's very pricey in Europe. I don't know how much a hairdresser would get paid. And...and we can't afford tickets, and I guess you need bleddy visas and things...' her voice trailed off. She sighed, and stirred the yellow mess of rice and lentils on her plate. Uff men! Life was so unfair.

∽৯

Jessica looked at her rectangular, twenty-eight-year-old body in the mirror and made a face. She was fit and strong, she could carry all the groceries up six flights of stairs in one go, but what did that matter if no suitor would ever look at her thick calves? She pulled her slip over her head, then bent and began undoing the buttons on her freshly ironed frock as it lay on the bed. Mrs Charles always did all the fastenings up when she sent Jessica's clothes back from her tiny laundry behind the house, bless her heart.

Hmmm, what about young Bill, Mrs Charles's nephew? Nah, just barely turned eighteen and already up to monkey business. She sighed. Some of the younger ones were dreamy, until they opened their mouths. But she was too old for them.

'There must be something better than this,' she said to her reflection. Her own face looked skeptically back at her. Not fooling anyone, am I? And there was Amelia to consider.

Jessica heard voices in the passageway and quickly finished putting on her frock. Damn, visitors now? She'd be late for work. But when she came out into the tiny corridor that she called the 'dining room' she saw it was only Mrs Silveira from next door. 'Just came to borrow a couple of eggs, dear,' she wheezed. 'Got anything in yer dooly?' Jessica sighed gustily and opened the cabinet by the door. Mrs Silveira was always 'borrowing' food. She'd show up, grab a whole bag of sugar and then sidle over in the evening with a pathetic samosa on a plate. She wasn't exactly starving; she survived on the rent from the crumbling house across the way, but she hated to eat alone. She'd had twelve children before her husband died, and they were all abroad. When they could, they sent money home.

Amelia was drawing imaginary pictures on the table with the end of her spoon. Mrs Silveira tucked herself into a chair and poked a finger into the greasy packet in the middle of the table. It contained one soggy jalebi from the shop on the corner and some biscuit crumbs. Jessica dumped the contents on a plate and put the two eggs in the bag for Mrs Silveira to take home with her. No chance of a proper breakfast now. Jessica took a big handful of roasted chickpeas from the enamelled tin over the stove. The sound of them cracking between her teeth was like gunshots.

Mrs Silveira picked at the syrupy biscuit crumbs as Jessica took a pan of milk out of the fridge and warmed a cupful over the one-ring stove. 'Jessica dear, are you going to the wedding?'

'What wedding, men? Does anyone even bother with wedding-shedding these days? As if there are any boys left.'

'Hehehe, what do you know, Jessica? The Caron boy is getting married.'

Jessica nearly spilled the milk she was pouring for Amelia. 'Whaat? Robert?' Another eligible bachelor down. 'Is he finally marrying Sarah Reynolds?'

'If only,' Mrs Silveira shook her white head. 'You know, the boy was holding out on us! Apparently he's had a girlfriend the whole time he was at college. A Bengali!'

'A Bengali?'

'Heheh, yes, a brainy girl too. Doing her PhD and all. Imagine!'

'Imagine!' echoed Amelia in exactly the same tone as Mrs Silveira, all the while circling a finger around the rim of the glass of milk.

'Why? Are there no suitable girls among us?' Jessica's eyes flashed. 'How will we survive if our own boys run after Bengali PhDs?'

'Caron Caron Caron!' Amelia warbled. 'Don't they have a big house by the river, up in Chandannagar? I saw it once when we went on that trip and all.'

'Bleddy liar, Amelia!' Jessica stared at her. 'You've never been to Chandannagar.'

'Yes I have. The King of the Fairies took me on his houseboat.'

'Really?' Jessica growled. This news about Robert had definitely soured her mood. 'Did he give you a big kiss afterwards?'

'No, he didn't, because everybody knows that if the fairies kiss you, you go mad.' Amelia slurped her milk and went on speaking through her broad milk moustache. 'And I'm quite sane, thank you very much.'

'They do have a big house by the river,' said Mrs Silveira. 'But Robert's getting married here, in Calcutta. At Dalhousie Club! Her family's throwing a big party for all the Anglos who can make it.'

'Fancy, eh? Is she rich?' Jessica asked nonchalantly.

'No, but they want to do the right thing.' Mrs Silveira said with prim approval.

'Hah! As if! Why aren't they having a church wedding? Christ the King is just a hop away up the road from Dalhousie. She's converting, right?' Jessica leaned forward expectantly.

'She won't. She has Views, I hear. Mae Simpson said, she knows the family.' Mrs Silveira nodded sagely.

'I'm sure the Lord has Views too, but do these people care?' Jessica grumbled.

Mrs Silveira patted Jessica's shoulder. 'You'll find someone, my girl,' she crooned soothingly, and shambled off back to her flat.

~~~

The card came addressed to 'Freddie Rosario and family'. It was suitably gold-edged, with embossed wedding bells. She scowled at it.

'Ooooh!' squealed Amelia, and ripped it from her hands. 'Wedding bells, wedding bells, wedding bells!'

'We're not going,' Jessica growled, 'This is not the kind of behaviour we should encourage in the community.'

'It's at Dalhousie Club! Beef kabab rolls and swings!' Amelia said excitedly.

'I haven't been there in years. Not since Keith left for

Kenya.' Jessica's eyes clouded at the memory.

'Keith?' Amelia frowned.

'Keith Abraham. Before your time. You were in Mrs Pereira's montessori school when I went on my first date. I was just eighteen, I had dreams to spare.' She chuckled wryly at the memory. 'Keith, well, he was never going to take me with him, bleddy basket. Anyway, we've not got anything to wear.'

'Yes we do. Our Sunday best!' Amelia did a little shimmy. 'What's good enough for God is good enough for man.'

'You're doolally, child,' said Jessica without heat. 'Why this sudden enthusiasm for Robert Caron's wedding? You never want to go anywhere.' She picked up her teacup and sipped it, pinky extended in ladylike fashion.

Amelia stopped dancing around and looked at her slyly. 'To give you an excuse to go.'

Jessica almost spat out her tea. 'What?'

'Come on, Jess-Jess. You know you want to.'

Jessica wiped her chin. 'One of these days,' she muttered, 'I'm going to give you such a *jhaaping*…'

But Amelia had waltzed off to the bedroom she shared with her big sister, to rummage in trunks and suitcases for the perfect outfit. Jessica followed, and after a while she caught her mood, and they were soon happily pulling out gowns that had belonged to Mamma and had somehow escaped becoming pawnshop fodder for

Florian's various bad habits. The dresses were all far too archaic to be worn to any occasion other than a fancy dress ball, but maybe Mrs Charles could alter them a bit, if her old eyes were up to it.

Amelia promised to ask her, and Jessica went off to work the next day with very mixed feelings. She still felt that Robert, whose father had been a merchant navy captain, ought to be setting an example to the other young men. Love was a poor foundation for something as heavy as family, she thought as she watched Rosy feeding rice and milk to her nine-year old son by hand. How long would romance last when surrounded by screaming, sticky, whiny kids? Social obligation had a broader back, in her opinion. Nothing like the disapproval of neighbouring aunties to keep a couple straight in their beds.

When she came home, two perfect gowns were laid out on the broken-down cane sofa next to the dining table, one sunset pink, for Amelia, and one tender green for Jessica. Mrs Charles had even noticed where Jessica had strained the seams when trying her dress on, and had discreetly inserted panels to accommodate her straight-up-and-down figure. Jessica couldn't help it—she melted. And Amelia was gleeful as a kitten with a ball of wool.

'So we're really going?' Jessica asked.

Amelia took her hands and waltzed her around the room. 'Yes, Jess, you *shall* go to the ball!'

'Shefali weds Robert', said the standee outside the venue in curly gold letters. Inside, tables were laid out in the tennis court. The aunties sat in a row, their hats nodding like flying saucers at a UFO convention. There was Auntie Mae and Auntie Alice and Auntie Helen and Auntie Pamela and Auntie Marilyn, all smelling of mothballs and jasmine attar.

'Jessica!' Auntie Helen crowed. 'Come here girl, give us a good look at you.'

Awkwardly clutching her bouquet of a dozen red roses (the card had said no gifts), Jessica allowed herself to be handed down the line. Amelia had run to the playground behind the gracious old clubhouse the moment they'd entered. Now Jessica could hear the swings creaking their protest in the children's area. Pretty soon the bearers would tell Amelia she was too old to play on them, and there would be sulking. Till then, Jessica smiled for the shortsighted old ladies, who were in the middle of an extended discussion as to who she resembled. Since their collective memories covered almost a century, this process would probably take some time.

Out of the corner of her eye she could see the glitter and colour of the Bengali contingent, dressed in their best Benarasi silks and clustered around the happy couple. Only Robert's head and shoulders were visible as he towered over the rest. He was looking down and speaking tenderly to someone she couldn't see—probably Shefali.

There were only about twenty of the 'other kind' as she thought of them, in contrast to the fifty or so Anglo-Indians present. Probably not all of the latter were wedding guests—some, she suspected, were club regulars who'd crashed the party, but the bride and her family seemed quite happy to host them all. There was Uncle Teddy, stuffing his face with fish fries in the corner, next to Old Pete who had forgotten his dentures and was slurping the *consomme* most distressingly.

A waiter was going around with whiskey and rum— she took a glass of Blender's Pride and watched the guests. Ah, that short dark girl in the red silk sari with the funny white tiara must be Shefali, the bride. The girl sitting next to the bride was much more glamourous. She had long dark silky hair falling in a river over her shoulders. Jessica squinted—the girl was wearing her sari in the Maharashtrian fashion, with the pleats tucked up between her legs like trousers. These fancy people: what will they think of next. As the aunties sank into their memories and forgot all about Jessica, she sidled over to greet the couple and hopefully get rid of the roses. Robert smiled at her and waved. She blushed—she'd never really exchanged a word with him, only met him every year at Christmas Mass at St Paul's. But his smile seemed genuine.

'Thank you so much!' Shefali took the dozen red roses bought at Beck Bagan Market as if they were precious jewels. 'You're Jessica? Pleased to meet you!' Some more young people arrived and squealed at Shefali's friend in the Maharashtrian sari. They made her get up and twirl so they could admire her. Jessica shook her head sadly: such a glamourous outfit, and the girl hadn't even bothered to thread her lip properly. Jessica's fingers clenched with professional discomfort.

And now Robert was being introduced to the new arrivals, who twittered and squawked in Bengali like exotic parrots. Jessica decided she'd done her duty. Best to go grab Amelia before she got up to mischief. She turned to go and found herself face to face with the hairy-lip girl. Oh horrors, she had chin-hair too. No, she was… he was…

Jessica couldn't help it. 'You're a m-!' She couldn't say the word.

'A model? Of course.' The person smiled sunnily, revealing perfect teeth. 'Do you like this outfit? It's by my friend Farhana. She's a designer, she did Shefali's outfit as well. My name's Rasheed, by the way. And you are?'

'J-Jessica. But…you're wearing a…and makeup… and…' Jessica stuttered.

'Well, I couldn't very well pair this outfit with a bit of lipgloss and a nose stud, could I?' Rasheed smiled. 'Had to do the whole fig.'

'But why didn't you thread your lip and wax your cheeks?' she asked, her voice trembling.

Rasheed looked shocked. 'Why would I do that?'

Jessica turned red under her tan. 'I'm a stylist. I know how to groom people. And you...you're....' She pulled herself together. 'If you want to dress as a woman, at least do a good job of it.'

Rasheed frowned in puzzlement. 'But I'm just dressed as me,' they said. 'I'm not imitating anyone.'

Shefali turned to them, smiled, got up off her chair and joined them. 'I couldn't help hearing,' she said. 'Jessica, Rasheed promised me they'd give me moral support, because I feel like I'm in drag in this outfit.' She laughed gently, spreading her hands to take in the deep scarlet silk with spangled borders. 'They're so much better at this than I am.'

Jessica looked helplessly from one to the other, 'I didn't understand a word of that sentence, y'all. Are you laughing at me?'

'Not at all,' Rasheed said seriously. 'You're a stylist, Jessica. I bet you do wedding makeup all the time.'

Jessica had to smile too, although a bit wryly. 'Every day during the season, men. Or it feels like it.'

'So you know that you can turn a mousy girl into a princess with just a few pastes and powders. That's the magic of art. All you need is a face to be your canvas. Doesn't matter whose face it is.' Rasheed fluttered their eyelashes. 'But it helps if your subject is willing to play their part and live up to your vision.'

'That's true,' Jessica said slowly. Then she looked past Shefali and saw Amelia approaching with a face like thunder. 'Oh dear,' she said. 'I think my sister's been turfed off the swings. Amelia! Over here!'

Amelia mooched up. 'I told them I'm eight but they wouldn't buy it.'

'You're fourteen, you junglee child.'

'Not in my head.' She looked Rasheed up and down. 'Hi.'

'Hello there, beautiful.'

'I like you.' She grabbed Jessica's whiskey before she could be stopped and tossed it off in one gulp. 'Ah! Now I don't care about the bleddy swings. Are those kababs? I want!' Jessica watched helplessly as Amelia locked onto the buffet.

'She's an original, your sister,' said Shefali.

'That she is,' said Jessica with feeling. 'She once told me she'd decided not to grow up, because it's obviously a trap.'

'Smart girl,' said Rasheed.

'No, she's just touched in the head.' Jessica looked at them both. 'You people are so weird.'

'That's an honest observation,' said Robert heartily, putting an arm round his new wife. 'It's all a matter of perspective, dear Jessica.'

'Every smart person worth their salt gets called a weirdo at least once in their life, *n'est-ce pas, mon cher*?' said Shefali.

The waiter came around again. They all took drinks. 'Here's to weird smart people!' said Robert. Jessica raised hers along with all the rest. Why the hell not. By the end of the evening she was pleasantly drunk, or at least tipsy enough to splurge on a cab instead of piling into a route 45 bus. Amelia snuggled into her side like a warm puppy.

'Did you have fun?' Jessica asked, and felt Amelia nod. Then the child spoke. 'I had more fun than I've had in my entire life.' And Jessica knew her sister well enough to know it wasn't hype. She meant it as fact.

'You know, I'm beginning to think I've got it all wrong,' Jessica said thoughtfully. 'I've been trying to put myself in a box made out of other people's bullshit expectations.'

'A box?'

'You know—be a good girl, do your duty, live the life you've been given, all that *bakwaas*.'

'Oh that. Huh.'

'Huh indeed.' Jessica looked down at her sister's dark head. 'But there will be changes now.'

'Good. It's about time.'

> **Author's Note:** This story is about a fast-vanishing community, the 'Anglo-Indians', who once brought their own special verve to the Kolkata scene. I say 'Anglo-Indians' because, as Jessica dimly senses at the beginning of the story, her community is actually far older than the advent of

the British in India. Originally called 'Eurasians', their roots stretch from Madagascar to Macao, Amsterdam to Amboyna, and their origins lie in the spice trade, which is at least three millennia old. Both the sun-browned and the winter-hardened genealogies among them often came from small maritime communities: Polynesian tribes, Fanqi Chinese, Armenian Jews, Peloponnesian Greeks, Basque and Maltese sailors, coastal Irish, French Huguenots, sea peoples of the Gulf.

Robert Caron's Franco-Bengali heritage lies in Chandannagar, as does Shefali Das's. Although Shefali is an ethnic Bengali, her background is as French as that of any cultured mademoiselle, since Frenchness for the tiny Chandannagar community lies in understanding the rights and duties of a *citoyen(ne)*, reading and admiring the literature and speaking the language flawlessly. It is ironic, therefore, that the more racially mixed Eurasian characters in the story initially regard her with suspicion.

Many Eurasians were hairdressers like Jessica, or dressmakers like her friend Mrs Charles, because the community's international connections meant they had a finger on the pulse of global fashion, and they brought a cosmopolitan spice to Kolkata's smart set. Their English is unique because they accepted all inputs. The ubiquitous 'men' (their pronunciation of 'man', used more or less like punctuation in their speech) seems to be derived more from the Scots usage than the Black American, as the Scots pronunciation (mon) is closer. Running schools was also a Eurasian thing because they were often versatile linguists, and they not only taught the children their idiosyncratic diction, but also their culture. In their own way, they were social entrepreneurs, and it is very sad that they have dispersed so thoroughly among the people of the world that their culture is fading, and the comparative poverty of those who are left means that they are too busy surviving to preserve what's left of their glory days.

The term 'bleddy basket,' as anyone who's ever studied in an Anglo school will know, is their pronunciation of 'bloody bastard.' Like every community, they also had their sketchy types, who are represented as minor characters here, but sketchy or not, they were never boring. Dalhousie Club, now known as Dalhousie Institute, welcomed everyone, and in its heyday you could walk in at any hour and find a dozen bon vivants of all genders propping up the bar and telling salty stories about their relatives from all around the world. They will be missed.

The Shelf Life
Aniket Majumdar

July was the cruelest month in Phoenix. The mercury climbed to shocking heights, unthinkable in the deceptively balmy months of April and May. Pathik's itinerant feet brought him to this city twenty years ago—after he had completed his graduate school in South Carolina. Unlike New York City or Kolkata where you could explore the city on foot, Phoenix was different. Hiking was possible, but that needed more conditioning. In peak summer, Pathik resorted to gardening. He had to be extra attentive to keep the *Malabar spinach* and *Rajanigandha* bushes alive in the sun-dried climate. He planted those in flower pots two springs ago and they had survived one summer already. Pathik was hopeful.

Ah Kolkata! 'The big dizzy', a city of 10 million. Pathik loved to walk on the streets of the city ever since he was allowed to do so on his own. His wanderings along the streets of Kolkata had now been glorified as heritage tours. His favourite walking challenge was the 14-kilometer route from *Baghbajar* to *Golpark* or even beyond to *Jadavpur*, which he hoped to complete in a day someday. Sometimes on shorter jaunts, when he negotiated the jostling crowds of *Rajabajar* or *Manicktala* or *Sealdah*, he marveled at the gall of his uncle Gaur, who when only nine years old, boarded the *Dhaka Mail* from *Pangsha*, his ancestral village in East Bengal, and managed to reach Rajabajar. The year was 1942. Miraculously, a family friend spotted Gaur in the city and brought him back home. This story was part of Pathik's family lore. And Pathik was touched by that wanderlust.

Last December, Pathik had flown in from Phoenix to be with his parents for a few days. One morning, as Pathik pulled aside the flowery drapes to enter his father's room, an old black and white photograph of him with his father caught his eye.

The room where his father spent a lot of time these days had a sofa-bed, two small couches, a rectangular table with a glass top and a four-shelf bookcase packed with books—a few brand new, a lot more bought from the myriad second-hand book stores scattered around the city. His father spent his time mostly reading—

newspapers, magazines and books. But his eyesight was failing and that was a cause for concern for everybody.

The photograph was on the top shelf of the bookcase, where it had been kept for over four decades, encased in a metallic frame that had withered over the years. The glass cover had turned hazy but no dust had collected, thanks to the regular wipe down by his mother. At times, Pathik had seen the photograph being placed over the old and boxy analog television set in his parents' bedroom. From time to time it received scrutiny as a conversation item when folks came to visit—one or both his parents would launch into an explanation of why Pathik appeared to be on the verge of tears.

Pathik went back to that crisp December morning. The year was 1963. Pathik's mother helped him put on his favorite sweater—biscuit-colored with a brown collar, brown tips at the wrists and a six inch zipper on the front. As Pathik struggled with the zipper, his mother rubbed his face with *Boroline*, a popular local brand of moisturizing cream, and smeared some more on his perpetually chapped lips. On any other day, this ritual would irk Pathik to no end but today was different. Pathik was prepared to endure a lot for the trip he was about to take with his father. Earlier in the morning Pathik was given a bucket of lukewarm water to take a quick bath, which he did without whining. His father wore a freshly ironed white shirt and a sleeveless moss green cashmere cardigan. They boarded a city bus from the five-point crossing at *Shyambazaar* on the north side of the city, a confusing confluence of five busy streets that kids were not allowed to go to on their own. Just coming to the five-point crossing would have been an adventure in itself for him.

The bus negotiated the Saturday morning traffic sporadically spewing diesel fumes. It stopped every quarter mile or so, letting off and taking on a few passengers at a time. A half hour ride brought them to the *Esplanade*, which marked the city center. Pathik and his father got down and walked along *Chowringhee Road*, the main thoroughfare connecting the downtown to the southern part of the city. They walked past the *Metro Cinema*, a movie theater for Metro-Goldwyn-Mayer productions and a popular meeting point for people visiting this part of town.

Next door was the *Savoy Camera Stores*, their destination. They had come for a photo shoot, well, actually one portrait. The sole employee quickly put down his tea cup and set aside the morning newspaper when he saw them approaching, quite pleased to have his first customers of the day.

They were ushered into the 'studio', a dimly-lit back room. Powerful lights were switched on, his father was shown a few options for a backdrop, and he chose a plain looking one, quickly bypassing a few colorful ones—dark blue with silver stars, a crescent moon, a bunch of bright green flowers. Pathik was asked to stand on a footstool next to his father. Pathik was marveling at what looked like umbrellas when he heard his father say, 'Face the camera…look where he's pointing to.' The edge in his father's voice filled Pathik with shame and indignation and his eyes welled up for being scolded in front of a stranger. His seven-year old frame shrank. Just then the shutter was pulled. 'Done,' said the photographer emerging from under a black cloak that had swallowed his head behind the box camera. 'You can pick this up on Monday afternoon,' the man informed his father. His father made sure the photographer knew that the family wanted a 5 by 7 print and then they left the store.

Outside the Savoy, a new world awaited Pathik. This was his first trip to the city center. Everything was a far cry from his familiar surroundings in Bagbazaar, with its narrow streets and cheek to jowl tenements. 'Let's take the tram,' his father said. As they headed back to Esplanade and the tram depot, his father pointed out some of the landmarks of the city, edifices built by the colonial rulers to resemble parts of nineteenth-century London. The street was getting more crowded now. Street vendors were laying out their wares on parts of the sidewalk. Small groups of people that looked like families, were milling about taking in the sights. Some of them were speaking in languages that Pathik didn't understand.

His father insisted Pathik hold his hand at all times. 'Do you see that tall column, that's the *Monument*.' Ten years later, Pathik learned it was the *Ochterlony Monument,* named after Sir David Ochterlony, the commander of the British East India Company forces in the Gurkha War of 1814. Kolkata has hundreds of monuments, some left over from the British period, but only that one is identified as the monument. Large political rallies are organized around the structure since the grounds can accommodate thousands of people. As a freshman in college, Pathik himself had his first feel of one such meeting at the foot of the Monument.

'You see the open area,' continued his father pointing south past the Monument at a vast grassy expanse. 'That's called the *Maidan*.' By then they had come to the tram depot, which had trams going in all directions, snaking around the crisscrossing tracks, the cables overhead looking just as messy. They waited at a stop and boarded the first compartment of a sleek southbound tram. Pathik's first tram ride. Many years later, Pathik would see similar streetcars in New Orleans.

His father let him have the window seat on the right side. They rode for some time along the length of the maidan, which seemed to stretch out for miles. The crisp and sunny December day was ideal for cricket matches. Teams of players of all ages occupied various patches of the ground, many even wearing the official all-white attire. His father pointed out the well-known affluent sports clubs that had cricket, football, hockey teams and had permanently fenced-off and gated enclosures. The ride seemed all too brief when his father indicated it was time to get off.

Once the tram moved on, another magical world opened up before Pathik's eyes. To their right lay the Maidan—lush green and seemingly endless, to their left was the bustling traffic on Chowringhee Road. His father drew his attention to what was ahead of them. 'Look over there, that's the *Victoria Memorial*.' Pathik had not seen any structure like it before, not even in books. The grounds of the memorial began close to where the Maidan ended. Two marble lions guarded its gate. Halfway in, there was an imposing statue of Queen Victoria and further down, the domed memorial building. There was a curious structure on top of the dome. Pathik read later that built with white marble to resemble the Taj Mahal, the memorial was built in honor of Queen Victoria, commissioned after her death by Lord Curzon, the then Viceroy of India. The structure on top was the rotating Angel of Victory.

Pathik was secretly hoping they would visit the memorial when his father took his hand and they crossed the tracks to go to the other side. 'We'll visit it some other time, when you are a little older,' his father assured him, as if reading Pathik's mind. Then his father let him in on a secret—Fort William, built by the British in the mid 1700s was entirely under the maidan. Just then a northbound tram arrived and they boarded it to head back to the Esplanade.

They got down after three stops and crossed Chowringhee Road to go to the east side. This time they took a busy side street and headed to what looked like a marketplace. There were a lot more street vendors and of course, more people. His father said there were people from many parts of the world here, some tourists, others whose ancestors came to the city a long time ago. 'They are going to *New Market*,' he announced. Originally coined *Hogg Market* in 1903, after Sir Stuart Hogg the then Commissioner of the Calcutta (Kolkata) Corporation, but the locals called it *New Market*, and the name stuck. New Market turned out to be a huge enclosure with a magnificent façade and several entrances. Inside there were shops of all kinds—flower shops, bakeries, china stores, clothing stores, bookstores, trinket stores, and even a section designated as the meat market.

They meandered their way to the bakery section. The aroma that greeted them was nothing Pathik was familiar with, and it was pleasantly comforting. Pathik looked at his father who was smiling down at him. Pathik noticed they had stopped in front of *Nahoum's Confectionery*, a pastry shop beyond compare. It was the holiday season and a great time for celebration, so the shop was crowded.

They had to wait a while to be served. 'Hold this carefully,' his father said handing him a white cardboard box, with Nahoum's written in blue on top. There were three kinds of pastries inside, each delicately placed in its own corrugated cupcake liner, the box tied with a blue ribbon, a special type of ribbon used by confectioners all over the city. Pathik would protect that treasure with his life, if need be. They left New Market and headed back to the Esplanade to catch the bus back home.

Thirty years later, on a December morning Pathik entered his father's room carrying a satchel with him. His father was trying to go through his ritual of reading four newspapers and did not look particularly happy, trying to read using the oversized magnifying glass Pathik had given him. His father went into a litany of ailments that bothered him as soon as Pathik sat on the couch facing his father. Pathik made the usual sympathetic noises to reassure his father. Pathik was looking at a man with wispy silver-grey hair and bushy eyebrows, a man who grew up near *Goalondo* in East Bengal, who had endured a lot in his lifetime—the Bengal Famine of 1942, the Partition of India in 1947 that made him and his family refugees, the loss of his mother from Cholera contracted from bathing in contaminated water, the death of all his three siblings, including one younger brother. He wanted to know where Pathik had been that early in the morning. Like a facile conjurer, Pathik dug inside his satchel and brought out a cardboard box tied with a blue ribbon. Pathik did not know how his father was going to react with all his myriad gastric discomforts.

Pathik's father took the box from him, closed his eyes briefly and inhaled deeply, and suddenly he was transformed into a young man in a green cashmere cardigan. What Pathik saw was his handsome face, his head full of wavy dark hair and the hint of a smile on his thin lips—all captured in that old photograph, and the image Pathik carried in his mind when his father was not with him. A box of pastries from Nahoum's, still occupying its place of pride in New Market and still run by one of the original, now octogenarian, Jewish owners, can take you back to your prime.

If you took the evening Dhaka Mail from Sealdah, you'd reach Goalondo by early morning. *Goalondo Ghaat* (landing wharf) was the gateway to ports and cities east and southeast along the Padma, places like *Chandpur, Naryanganj, Madaripur, Barisal.* Pathik wished he had taken that train trip to visit his ancestral village. He imagined walking among the ruins of the dwelling and the vast estate, walking past King George High School, which his father attended, and going up to the *Chandana* river. He'd occasionally encounter some locals, meeting his favourite personality the imaginary Karim. 'Karim Chacha,' he would call out. Pathik imagined Karim's weather-beaten face would open in an edentulous grin.

'Khoka babu, what brings you here?' Folks like Karim would tell him about the people who lived in these parts in the past, his father's extended family. His family's post-partition life began when they left behind the memory of the anadromous *ilish* (hilsa) and left for Kolkata in 1948. His father never took the train back, spending all his life in his adopted city. The Dhaka Mail stopped running in 1965. The shelf life of a photograph is measured in human years, perhaps the shelf life of memory is measured in human tragedies.

It is the end of July. Last night, it rained in parts of Phoenix, particularly the area where Pathik lives. It was evening and Pathik was returning from work. As he walked up to his front door, the fragrant whiff of the Rajanigandha reached him. True to its name, the flower that only releases its fragrance in the evening had blossomed on the stalks. Pathik had finally arrived home.

SECTION FOUR
REVOLUTION

Revolution
Soumitro Das

I found them in the guest room which had been locked ever since I moved into the new house. I had gone there to fetch my accordion. I opened the door and saw an old man with a beard, five or six children, aged between five and twelve and a young woman, docile and plain, with a veil thrown over her head, the old man standing up and looking at me in surprise, the children playing on the floor and the woman cooking over a charcoal stove, in a corner of the room.

I said, Who are you? What are you doing in my house?

The old man immediately fell at my feet, the woman sent up a loud wail, and the children bawled like a brood of banshees.

What is this? I said.

Babu, he said. We have nowhere to go. We have come from far. Everything we had is lost to the floods. We know no one in this city. So we took shelter here.

What do you mean? I said, scarcely able to believe what I was hearing. This is a private residence. You can't just walk in and take over the place. Leave immediately.

The old man fell at my feet and the woman sent up another wail.

Babu, said the old man, I have six children to feed. This is their mother. If you throw us out we will be reduced to begging for our lives.

I noticed a bottle of milk, some fruit rinds, a casserole of rice and some cooked vegetables in a pot, scattered on the floor. I also saw a tetra pack of orange juice that had obviously come from my refrigerator.

What? I said. You have been eating my food. How did you get into the kitchen?

The old man sobbed helplessly.

How did you get inside my house? I said, quite beside myself.

They all started weeping together, the children huddled and fearful, the woman inconsolable.

I noticed the window at the back. One of the panes was missing. All they had to do was thrust their hand inside and undo the latch. There was some old furniture in the room which they were using to sleep at night. I saw some spare articles of clothing, of a rural stamp, spread out over some sofas, for drying. These people had set up a regular establishment here, in my house.

I was furious.

I am going to call the police, I said.

The old man flung himself at my feet, grabbing them with both hands.

Babu, he whined piteously, please forgive us. We know it is wrong to enter somebody's house like this. It is a shameful trespass on our part. Spit on my old head a thousand times if you like. But think of these poor children and their mother, a defenceless woman abandoned by her husband. Where will they go, what will become of them?

How should I know? I shouted back at him, angrily. This is not a charity shelter.

Babu, the old man cried out. Please don't call the police. We will leave on our own.

Good, I said. Get out.

His bearing changed immediately to one of dignified sadness.

Give us some time to pack our belongings, he said.

Okay, I said. I'll be back in an hour. If I still find you here, I will call the police.

His body shook with convulsions of grief and despair.

I came back after an hour to find them gathered around an old couch, on which the young woman lay prone.

That's it, I said. I am going to call the police.

Babu, said the old man. The woman is too sick to be moved.

My eyes narrowed with suspicion.

She was all right an hour ago, I said.

I noticed the children had an imploring look in their eyes. Some of them had little glaciers of green and white snot running down their noses onto their upper lip.

The old man caught my glance and said, Think of these poor little children.

That's not my problem, I said. Get them all out of here. Go to a home for destitutes.

What is that? said the old man.

A shelter for the homeless, I said.

Yes, babu, said the old man eagerly, we shall go there as soon as possible. Only let us stay here for the night. Till the woman gets better. Then we shall go.

I raised my hands and let them drop in exasperation.

This is not possible, I said. This is my house, you understand? You are intruders. You have no right to stay here. I can call the police and have you thrown out.

One of the brats had attached himself to the old man's dhoti and was following the altercation with eyes dripping with fear.

The old man folded his hands and said, May God shower all his blessings on you for being merciful towards this woman and her poor, hungry children.

But, this is my house, I said, irritated beyond measure.

At this point, the woman on the couch, who had been shivering diligently, moaned, as if in pain. Her hands clutched the sheet which covered her, feverishly. I expected her to cough.

After a while she coughed.

I was being taken for a ride.

One of the children started wailing.

The woman is not ill, I said. She is faking it.

At this, the old man seized my right hand and said, Touch and see for yourself. She has fever.

He placed my hand on the woman's forehead. It was, indeed, burning.

I had been proven wrong.

The old man reading the contrition on my face, came forward eagerly.

You see, Babu, he said. She is ill. Cannot be moved.

Take her to a doctor, I said.

Tears trickled down the old man's cheeks.

We have no money, Babu, he said. It is already night. We don't know any doctors here. Let us stay here for the night. Tomorrow morning we will go away.

I clenched my jaws. I did not want them around. I did not like the old man, I did not like the children, I did not like the woman. They looked dishonest and purposeful. And yet, I was, all of a sudden, unwilling to call the police. Something inside me baulked at the idea of throwing a sick person out of my house. Ordinary human decency.

All right, I said. Tomorrow morning by eight o clock. Otherwise I call the police.

This was already the third time I had threatened to call the police. The menace in the phrase was being eroded through repetition.

No sooner had I said this than the children stopped crying and the woman, shivering. The old man placed his hand on the head of a child hidden in the folds of his dhoti and said, I swear on the forehead of this child, by tomorrow morning, we shall be gone.

I heaved a sigh of relief and returned to my room.

The next morning, I found them as entrenched as I had left them the previous evening. They had washed up and were wearing new clothes. Their belongings were scattered all over the place. There was no sign of an imminent exit.

The old man was standing, in the middle of the room, with a slightly querulous expression on his face.

I went straight to the phone and rang up the local police station. The OC came over immediately.

Illegal entry and theft, I said, Take them in.

Wait, said the old man.

He reached into the pockets of his upper garment, drew out a piece of paper and handed it over to the OC.

It says here, said the old man, pointing out the writing

on the paper with his long, knobbly forefinger, that we are the real tenants of this property. We came here this morning and found this man occupying our property. We were about to go to the police station.

The OC looked at the paper, then at the old man and then at me.

What! I said. What is this paper?

The OC showed it to me.

It was a receipt, made out in my name, by the landlord, for six months rent in advance.

But this is my receipt, I said. Here, see, this is my name at the bottom. I moved in last month. I left it in the drawer of a desk which is inside this room.

The man is lying through his teeth, said the old man, firmly. I signed an agreement with the landlord two months ago. We arrived here today to take possession of the flat and found this man living here. We were about to come to you to register an FIR. Please throw him out.

I took out my wallet and fished out my driving licence.

See, I said, holding it up for the OC to see, it's the same name.

The OC looked at the old man.

That means nothing, said the old man indifferently. He can have the same name. It is not such an uncommon name.

The OC looked at me.

But, I said, this is preposterous!

The OC said, Let's call up the landlord and find out who is speaking the truth.

The OC picked up the phone and dialed the number printed on the receipt.

The conversation went something like this.

Hello! I want to speak to Mr_ Hello! Hello! I want to speak to Mr_ Hello! Yes! I want to speak to Mr_ He's not in town?...Mombassa...When will he be back?...Not for another year...Can I have his address?...I am the OC of X police station...there is a dispute regarding the renting out of one of his properties...No, I'd rather speak to him personally...Yes... just hold on...

The OC gestured to me to give him something to write on.

I handed him a piece of paper.

He scribbled down an address and put down the phone.

I am sorry, he said, turning to me, the landlord is in Mombassa and won't be back for another year. Is there any other way you can establish that your claim on this property is sound?

I had just moved in. I hadn't had the opportunity of paying any bills, electricity, telephone, etc. I had no ration card. Didn't need one.

That receipt is mine. I put it in the desk which I don't use so I moved it in here. I didn't know I was going to face such a situation.

The OC looked at me sympathetically.

I suggest, he said, you write to the landlord. Here is the address. Get an affidavit, with your picture attached, identifying you as the tenant, go to court, get an eviction order and then come to me. We'll do the rest.

But that will take weeks, maybe months! I said.

The OC sighed. There was a look of commiseration on his face.

I am sorry, he said. There is no proof that that receipt is yours. Legally, as of now.

So, what am I supposed to do, I said, casting a wild glance at the bunch of creatures in the guest room.

The old man stood there, watching the proceedings impassively. The young woman sat on the couch, veil drawn over her face.

As I was saying, said the OC, write straightaway to the landlord.

A court order, I said, my voice grown shrill with nervousness. What am I supposed to do with these people?

The OC looked at me sadly.

I am sorry, sir, he said. I can't do anything. My hands are tied.

But this is a criminal trespass, said I.

You will have to prove it in a court of law, sir, he said, his expression conveying a deep understanding of the pathos and the gravity of my predicament.

You mean, I'll have to allow these people to live here?! In my flat?!

The OC said nothing.

I looked at the intruders in horror.

As soon as you get a court order, the OC said quietly, we'll evict these people.

And then, he left.

The old man stepped forward and slammed the door of the guest room shut on my face. I caught a glimpse of the children looking at me, shamefully, fearfully, uncomprehending the hatred the world held for them.

I spent the night, tossing and turning in my bed, unable to sleep. Suddenly made aware of their presence, I could now hear them talking in the other room. I felt a wild and uncontrollable rage. I could do nothing. I, who had been brought up to believe that something could always be done. Foul thoughts ran through my head. Should I rough the old man up? But having been given a glimpse of the law's ambiguity and the ruthless cunning of the old man, I was wary of taking any precipitate action against these creatures. That piece of paper had stopped the police in its tracks. Maybe I should hire some hoodlums. Thus, I oscillated between my law-abiding conscience and the truth that was mocking at me, in my own house.

The next day I went to see a lawyer, got an affidavit

typed, affixed a picture and posted it to Mombassa.

I went back to my flat to find somebody using my shower.

I banged on the door.

You can't use my shower, I shouted.

The old man emerged from the guest room and cool and impassive said, Who says we can't?

I stared at him in disbelief

Where are we supposed to wash ourselves? he continued. In the street? Legally, for the moment, this house belongs as much to me as to you.

You will stay in that room, I said, and not move out, until I get this matter sorted out at court. I had put my authority on the line.

It made no impression on the old man.

And if I don't? said the old man. What will you do? Call the police?

The children had gathered behind him and were looking on in interest. They looked more relaxed now. Something had registered in their brains.

They understood through the behaviour of the three adults that they had secured a slight advantage against this babu who, like other babus, under similar circumstances, wouldn't have let them cross the front porch. They were still there. The old man's demeanor told them that the time had not yet come to take further liberties in this strange new world of security and comfort.

You bastard! I said. You bastard!

A hint of a smirk played on the lips of the old man.

I was boiling over with rage.

Here was an enemy that was hiding in front of my eyes and telling me so.

He was proving himself to be much more of a man than I.

Meanwhile, the woman scurried out of the bathroom and into the guest room.

The sight infuriated me.

This peasant woman was already displaying a sense of familiarity with my living environment.

I will tell you what I am going to do, I said, looking at the old man with blind hatred. I am going to put all the rooms in this house under lock and key.

The expression on my face must have been impressive. The children looked subdued and even the old man was back to his circumspect self.

He said nothing. He went back to the guest room, children in tow, and shut the door.

Little lambs of satisfaction frolicked in my head.

I bought a set of locks and keys and locked up everything: the master bedroom, the study, the store room, the kitchen, the unattached bathroom which the woman had used and was smelling of hair oil and was in a mess, and even the doors that led to the balconies.

Some order had been restored. The law would take

its own course.

I went to office, secure in the knowledge that I had asserted my right to property.

I came back in the evening to find my living room in a mess. A vase lay smashed on the floor, as did the remains of an unspeakable gruel, there were one or two stains of betel juice on the wall and bidi butts in the ashtray. Clothes had been spread out to dry, on the dining table.

I went and banged on their door. Their door?

Open up! I shouted.

There were shuffling sounds inside.

The old man opened the door.

What is it? he said calmly.

You are not supposed to come into the living room, I said. Take these clothes off my dining table.

At least there could be no dispute about the furniture. It was mine.

The old man made a sign to the woman who quickly got up and picked up the clothes.

Next, I called up a security agency and ordered a guard for my living room.

At night, I lay in my bed, my head full of dark and improbable calculations. I would get rid of this nightmare, this cold-blooded agriculturist, who had barged into my life, with his litter of brats and now possessed of a legal right of abode in my house. I calmed myself with the thought that the affidavit from Mombasa would be here any day.

A week later, I found a brown paper envelope in my letter box.

It was not from Mombasa. It had a local stamp.

I opened it and found a lawyer's notice asking me to let his client, who had the same name as mine, to use the amenities in my property – address given – of which he was a legal tenant. Failing which, he would appeal to the appropriate court for the appropriate remedy.

My hands trembled as I read the notice, not out of fear, but out of surprise. How did this fellow get hold of a lawyer, a lawyer who spoke my language and not theirs? How did he know so much about the world and the tricks it permitted? This rustic son of a bitch was threatening to take me to court to assert his right over my property! No school I had ever been to had taught me such equations.

I sank into my upholstered sofa, too dazed to think.

The next day, I went to my lawyer.

Until we get the affidavit duly signed by your landlord, my hands are tied, he said.

What should we say in that case? I said.

He drafted a 'suitable' response to the effect that his client would assert his right before a court of law, in the not too distant future and, meanwhile, refused all discussion on the use of the property of which he is the legal tenant.

I wondered why the old man didn't go to the police and get an eviction order against me. What inhibited him? For all legal intents and purposes, he was the rightful tenant. He had the receipt. Not me. But, I looked the part, not he. Was that of any consideration under the law? I didn't know. But it seemed to count for something with the OC, which is what saved me I suppose.

Within a month, I received a copy of a court order saying that since the tenancy of the property was in dispute, the status quo must be maintained, that is, the parties would continue to occupy the portions that they now occupied and share the common spaces such as the living room, the unattached bathroom and the kitchen.

I was now seized with terror. In six weeks, this pasty-faced scoundrel, smelling of the earth and its labor, had swindled me out of a part of my rented accommodation. Were such things possible? Justice was blind? Could it not see the truth? That this humble farmer, or whatever profession he had followed before becoming a gate-crasher, was a petty cheat with glaciers flowing in his veins? I thought the world was Newtonian—every action had an equal and opposite reaction. But I heard the chief minister of one of our states use this phrase to justify a program.

I was, therefore, living in a world where Newton was open to interpretation? A world in which one hesitated to press the button for fear of summoning up fiends from the netherworld, instead of a solution to a problem.

I had pressed all the right buttons and this is what I had got.

I got hold of the landlord's phone number in Mombasa and called him up.

He was pleased to hear from me, he said. He had signed the affidavit and sent it back. I hadn't received it? That was strange. He asked me to send him another one along with the rent for the next six months. He would sign the affidavit and issue me a receipt and dispatch through courier to my lawyer.

I did not feel relieved. I was almost convinced that this old man, ruminating on betel leaves with the nonchalance of a cow, was the covert plenipotentiary of a gaggle of malicious spirits, out to rob me of my life.

How could a simple peasant get the better of me, a brilliantly educated man from a decent family, holding a job that required ruthlessness of judgment and tenacity of purpose, far above the ordinary, qualities in recognition of which I was handsomely compensated. I was supposed to win, he was supposed to lose. But it was I who was losing. Hands down.

All I knew now was that it was difficult to arrive at a correct estimate of the reserves of animal cunning that my adversary possessed and the extent to which he was willing to deploy them.

The entire episode had so far revealed only one trait in his character – inscrutability, the capacity for self-concealment.

This, in turn, gave rise to all kinds of suspicions.

What else could he do that I couldn't? What, for instance, had happened to the mail that my landlord had sent me? Had he pilfered it? But he couldn't know English and the letter box was impregnable. Was he in cahoots with the policeman?

I could not know. I had no answers for questions that were not even questions, but doubts, mere doubts, foreboding flickers in my brain.

I went to my lawyer, got another affidavit drafted and sent it off to Mombassa.

From that moment onwards, my life changed forever.

I now had to share my living space with a bunch of parasites, who did not belong to my set and about whose minds I knew nothing, excepting that its lack of scruple was frightening and that it wanted to feed on me.

II

The old man came up to me and said, I want our room cleaned up in the morning, like the rest of the flat.

I pay the maidservant, I said.

It's your flat, he said, mimicking the emphasis I used when talking to him. Don't you want to keep it clean?

I gave the relevant instructions to the maidservant.

After two days, she said she was quitting.

I asked her why.

She said she wasn't paid to clean up human excreta.

After this, I went through a succession of maidservants, none of whom lasted more than a week.

The old man came and spoke to me again. There was a slight change in his demeanor. An almost imperceptible change. The mask had taken on another shape. I could not put my finger on it.

Babu, he said, using the word he had first used on the dramatic night of discovery, but the attitude was no longer groveling.

I see you are having problems keeping your maidservants.

Then he pointed to the woman.

I saw immediately where he was going.

You must be out of your mind, I said, if you think I am going to employ any of you after what you have done. Besides, the maidservants leave because they find shit on the floor in that room.

They are lying! said the old man, his face suddenly taking on the expression of wounded pride, his voice rising in indignation. Because they don't want to do the extra work, that's all! You should raise their salaries and they will stay!

No, I said, I believe what my maidservants tell me.

Besides, I said, trying some of his own brand of irony on him, you are supposed to be the tenant, remember! How can your daughter work here as a maidservant?

I laughed.

The old man looked at me as if I had declared war on him.

Suit yourself, he said and went back to his room.

For the next one month, I tried to hire a maidservant, but none could be found. The word had spread that my flat was a pigsty.

I tried carrying on as bravely as I could.

But every evening I would come home to find leftovers, footprints and children's potty on the floor of the living room. Stoically, with a broom and a scuttle, I would clean the mess myself.

My parents had taught me well. They had taught me that life was full of adversities and that I should confront them with firmness and determination, not run away from them. But they hadn't told me I would have to clean up potty left behind by people whom I would normally employ as servants.

For the first time in many years, tears welled up in my eyes.

I had another altercation with the old man. He denied everything and accused me of littering my own drawing room in order to put the blame on him and his entourage.

Then, one evening, when I was trying to put my living room in order, the young woman came out, took the broom and scuttle from my hands and quietly went about finishing the job I had begun.

I let her.

I was letting her take my authority away from me.

Without a word being exchanged, the woman took over the responsibility of keeping my house clean. She was not rendering a service. She was simply exploiting the disadvantage that my upbringing had placed me in. She was destroying my sense of self.

Every morning, she would wake up and clean the house, before I left for office, locking the two rooms I used, behind me.

In the evening, I found the living room in perfect order. But it was no longer my living room. I was not sovereign.

The children understood this immediately. When they saw their mother going about the house, freely, without so much as a murmur of protest on my part, they knew the distance between their world and mine had been reduced.

When, in the evening, I sat down in front of the television, with a drink and some snacks, they would shyly come out of the guest room and assemble behind the sofa, all six of them. My first instinct was to chase them away. But my first instincts no longer counted. I reminded myself that the court order was explicit – the living room was to be shared between the parties in dispute. They had a right to be there. I could do nothing.

I could feel their alien presence behind me, there

was a hostile edge to that presence. They would talk in whispers. I could hear their tongues slapping against the palate, the saliva jostling around in their cheeks, a precocious hoarseness that comes from talking too much. When I switched to my favourite English movie channel, I would hear them trying to follow what was happening, in their own language. They couldn't follow much, but I could sense the wonder in their voices at a world that, obviously, could not exist for them as a reality, nor as a fantasy, but only as an oddity, like a three-legged baby, as a marvelous deformity for which no cure could be found. When a man and a woman kissed, they giggled.

I was part of the spectacle. They had stumbled upon a new specimen of humanity. They watched what I ate and drank, the way I lit my cigarette with my lighter, the way I manipulated the remote.

And they talked all the time, incessantly, hoarse whispers, clucking sounds, pronounced lisps, or, when there was violence, which they could follow easily, a barely articulated whisper against a backdrop of mouth breathing. The smallest among them, a black damnation with puffed up cheeks, always drooling, had the tip of her small, red tongue permanently exposed, between her slightly parted lips.

I would have felt nothing if I had seen them playing in the street, like other children of their kind. The repugnance that I felt was caused by social proximity. I felt them creeping all over me, threatening the boundary between me and them. The thought that they might consider me as part of their normal landscape, like a tree in a forest, and forget about me altogether, made me mad. This was my flat!

I could have easily shifted the television to my bedroom. But, I understood, correctly, this would be treated by the enemy as a retreat, emboldening him to take the offensive further. I was no longer watching television. I was defending territory. The territory of myness.

And yet, at the same time, the pride in my mind refused this war.

This wasn't the battlefield to which I was destined by my birth; this wasn't the enemy I had been brought up and trained to combat. I was supposed to fight my own kind, people of my set. This was not the territory I had to conquer and defend, my parents had already done that for me. To engage in hostilities with such an enemy, on his terms, that is, terms which I was not mentally equipped to meet, was to already accept that the life I had lived thus far, was false, that I had been walking through water and had left no trace behind.

I began drinking more than it was my habit to do just to be able to forget the vultures who whispered and shuffled behind me. And I did. To the point where I made my second act of submission.

This happened on a Sunday morning. It was a bright, sunny, winter day. I was sitting on the sofa, watching a cricket match on television, drinking beer and munching wafers. The old man whom I was forced by the law to call by the name my parents had given me, had just finished doing his morning prayers which was usually accompanied by a prolonged ringing of the bell and blowing of a conch shell. The woman had finished cleaning up the house. The children had been unleashed into the living room, but television sedated them partially. Birds were chirping in the air, there were the usual street sounds – some traffic, some hawkers, scraps of conversation.

I was almost feeling like myself – a senior corporate executive, relaxing on Sunday morning, after a hard week's work.

Suddenly, a black rubber ball rolled into the area where I was sitting. I heard some whimpering behind me, followed by a whispered consultation between several voices, which, by the tone, suggested that someone was being goaded into doing something.

After some time, I felt the presence of something black and small, just next to the sofa. I turned my head towards it to find the little girl standing there, looking at the black rubber ball which was hers and I understood that she was afraid of crossing my line of vision, crossing the border between herself and myself.

The eyes wide open, black and still that seemed to

diminish her flat nose even further, the red tip of her tongue exposed by the slightly parted lips, she stared at me, unsure of what I might do, if she went for her property.

As I said, I was feeling relatively secure that morning. I felt more like a master in my own house.

Take it, I said, in her language.

She continued staring at me. The fact that I had granted recognition, first to her presence in what she knew, in her own obscure way, was my flat, second to her right to take back her ball from an area clearly demarcated in her mind, as belonging to me, was taking time registering in her brain, so scared was she.

There was some prompting from behind the sofa.

The meaning of the signs I had made, in her language, were being confirmed for her by those who understood them better.

The little girl rushed forward to take hold of the ball.

It was at that point that something gave way inside of me. Maybe it was the beer.

I felt pity. Watching that little girl who had invaded my home from another world of which I knew now a little more than my peers, but which remained fundamentally alien, rush, with ungainly steps towards the ball and pick it up, was, for me, a pathetic sight. It suddenly dawned on me: these people had so little, I had so much. So great was the distance between our two worlds, that in spite of the pressure being exerted by theirs on mine, I was still capable of thinking in this way.

A little smile appeared on her face when she got her ball back. It was a smile of happiness. She looked, not at me, who had allowed all this to happen, but toward her siblings, seated behind me on the floor.

This was a child, not an enemy troop.

My parents hadn't taught me this.

I said, Come here, beckoning to her with my fingers.

She stopped in her tracks, caught in the same dilemma that had prevented her from moving into my territory. She understood the words, spoken in her own language, without understanding their meaning. She was not sure what those words meant in the world I lived in.

I had to repeat myself.

She stood rooted to the spot, staring at me as if I had uttered a threat. I saw she was on the verge of tears.

I smiled to reassure her. But I didn't know what my smile meant in her world.

The red tip of her tongue disappeared for a second into the surrounding blackness and reappeared again. But she did not move.

I picked up a wafer from the barquette lying in front of me and offered it to her.

There was pin drop silence behind me. Hostile silence. These movements were unexpected and, therefore, suspicious. I was the enemy.

The little girl started bawling her guts out. She thought I was about to do something dreadful.

I was a little flustered by her reaction. I was afraid the mother would come rushing out and hurl some awful accusation at me.

But nothing happened.

In their world, I thought, children cry all the time and are paid no attention. They are expected to inure themselves against pain and fear.

I went up to the girl and held the wafer under her nose. She let out a shriek that surprised me by its loudness.

At this point, the mother came out of the room and rushed towards her daughter, looking at me, eyes flashing with anger and suspicion. She asked the child what had happened. The child couldn't say anything, she was crying with all the energy her little body possessed. She asked the child if I had beaten her. More crying.

I intervened and said, as gently as I could, I was trying to give her this wafer.

The mother looked at the wafer with suspicion, as if it was poison.

She took the child away without uttering a word.

This episode had unexpected consequences.

The voices behind the sofa grew imperceptibly louder. The tone, too, had changed. Imperceptibly. From speculative to affirmative. I felt they had begun assigning meanings to the world that lay beyond the sofa.

I, too, had changed. Imperceptibly. Since the state of hostilities between us lay frozen by the court order and since our areas of sovereignty had achieved some sort of a stable demarcation, there were no more quarrels, only a tense cohabitation.

I soon got used to watching television with six poor children sitting behind me and talking incessantly in whispers. Despite all the unpleasantness, I empathized with them. The old man is the devil, I said to myself. In a few days, my lawyer would receive the papers from Mombassa and I would throw the bastard out. But I had no quarrel with the children. They were innocent. I was going to win anyway, the law would ultimately take my side, the side of the truth. All this was just a temporary inconvenience.

So, after a reasonable lapse of time, I called the girl again. She hesitated at first but, after some encouragement from others, she came up to me, where I was sitting on the sofa, the rubber ball in her hand and looked at me, with her still, black eyes. I took a biscuit and held it out for her. She hesitated. Once again, it was not the thing that amazed her, even she understood it was a trifle, but the person making the gesture. The biscuit was being dropped into her waiting palms from an immense, godlike height. This time, however, she let the ball drop from her hands and took the biscuit and then ran back to her place behind the sofa, happy.

The voices behind me grew even louder.

I had the situation under control. I dealt with them the way a suburban property owner would deal with his gardener's children, with impersonal benevolence.

Soon, I was sharing all kinds of tit-bits with them. I took care never to offer them kebabs or cocktail sausages, because, one, they might be vegetarians, two, it would have been overgenerous on my part, thoroughly confusing all their calculations with regard to me and engendering responses that I might not have been able to predict, nor to control.

I wanted to limit any familiarity to the one that could exist between subordinates and superiors. My worldly instincts were back in order.

They would now ask me to explain to them what was happening on television and I would explain it to them. They were happy I was talking to them normally. It lifted the oppressive cloud we were all under. They were more oppressed than I for they knew they were in the wrong. It was only the old man's iron will and implacable hostility that was keeping them there. They discussed my explanations among themselves and tried to match it with what they saw.

Their voices too had grown distinct, more individualized. It was no longer tongues slapping against the palate, or the barely audible popping sound made by lips parted and let through tiny volumes of air that they, because of their permanently slackened jaws held always in their mouths, or the smacking sound made by a tongue disengaging itself from the palate, bathed in saliva, sounds that I found disagreeable. They came from a world where one could hear the organs of speech as well as the speech itself.

Now a new element had been introduced. Laughter. The degree of enjoyment they derived from television had gone up. I had to tell them to lower their voices, but I noticed that they did not have as much control over their vocal chords as people like us did, they could either whisper or talk loudly, there were no intermediate decibel levels. They came from a rudimentary world where there were only a certain number of social situations. The voices grew louder despite my admonition, despite their willingness to listen to me.

Thus it was. Until Reshmi arrived on the scene one morning.

III

Reshmi was my fiancé and the only person to whom I confided all my troubles. My parents were dead. An elder brother worked in Australia. I was new to this town and knew no one apart from my colleagues. I had told Reshmi nothing because the problem had become too serious to bother someone I loved with. I would tell her when the whole thing had blown over.

Reshmi arrived one Sunday morning, without warning. She said she just wanted to be with me, but later on, after ascertaining the situation I was in, confessed that she had sensed all was not right with me, it showed in our telephone conversations.

I was watching television and the children were all in the hall as usual. She hugged me first and then, taking the children to be my servants' children, smiled at them.

The children looked astonished, sullen and uncomfortable.

With the keen eye that life demanded of them they realized that they had been shut out of my life. The new person had a stronger claim over me than they had and her gravitational pull might have a certain impact on my relationship with them.

Reshmi was nonplussed by their reaction, but, not being aware of what was going on, put it down to shyness.

I was not entirely happy about her sudden appearance. I didn't want her to get involved in all this – it was too crass for her. My reaction to her hug was inhibited by the awareness that the children were watching and judging as they would a man and a woman hugging on the television screen, with coy amusement. In reality, such an act would be taken as an act of cultural aggression. Reshmi noticed that I was inhibited and asked me what the matter was. I picked up her suitcase, took her by the arm and hastily bundled her into my bedroom. Out of the corner of my eye, I saw the children scurrying back into the spare room, like troops withdrawing upon the arrival of enemy reinforcements.

I explained the whole situation to Reshmi.

The frown on her face cut deep furrows on her forehead.

And so, she said, after I had finished recounting my story, you just have to put up with these people until this letter or whatever arrives.

Yes, I said.

This is absolute nonsense, said Reshmi, in her usual forthright manner.

Yes it is, I said.

The expression on her face grew darker and darker. With Reshmi, anger was of the slow and durable variety. She was the daughter of a high court judge with some wealth on her mother's side. In the hierarchy of doers, she was situated, a little above me and was, therefore, less likely to be tolerant of such facts than I was.

Something has to be done, she said. This can't go on.

There is a court order, I said.

I don't give a fig for court orders, said Reshmi. There was a hard, cold look on her face and I knew trouble was brewing.

I am going to call papa, she said.

She picked up the phone and called her father. She spoke to him for about an hour. From her side of the conversation I understood that legal options were being explored and also the possibility of getting in touch with senior police officers and other officials in my town, on whom her father could exert considerable influence. Her father said I could appear against the court order in a higher court. This option had already been rejected by my lawyer who said it would take as much time as presenting the affidavit and getting an eviction order. Her father promised to speak to some people he knew in my town. Reshmi passed the receiver on to me. Her father had the kind of voice that people who take their authority for granted have. It was gentle, soothing, reassuring. He was fond of me and genuinely sorry. He asked me not to worry and said the problem would be sorted out.

When the conversation was over, Reshmi put her arms around me and said, Don't worry, darling, everything will be all right. But she looked unhappy and I was unhappy because she was. The suffocation, the sense of being confined, of dealing with a hostile entity, that I had temporarily managed to dispel, was back.

At night, we made love, but it was a sham. We were both self-conscious, we felt we were being watched by hostile, prying eyes, who resented the joy we took in each other, feared that it might rebound on them. They knew I was no longer alone. Their hostile awareness was seeping through the walls of the bedroom.

This made Reshmi even more furious. My world was

her world and anything that damaged my sovereignty damaged her as well.

I am not going to put up with this nonsense anymore, she said, staring straight and hard at the ceiling.

What can we do? I said.

I don't know, said Reshmi. If I see them I am going give them a piece of my mind.

The next morning, the young woman did not come out of her room to clean the flat. It was quiet.

I decided to take a week off from work to be with Reshmi. She wanted to go out and see the town, do some shopping and, above all, escape.

We got dressed up and ready, when she asked me, What about your maidservant?

I told her.

What?! she said. You employ one of them to clean up your place?

Her eyes spoke, they said, what kind of a man are you?

I explained to her the chain of events that had forced me into this shameful compromise.

Her look changed immediately to one of anxious commiseration.

Oh my God! she said. These people are absolutely horrible.

It was then that she declared war on them.

She went up to their room and banged on the door.

The old man opened the door. The change in his demeanor when he saw Reshmi was remarkable. Here, I must add, that Reshmi was not only pretty but had the stylish, no-nonsense air that came with her upper middle-class background. The look on her face was like thunder. I saw the old man intimidated for the first time since I saw him. His instincts immediately told him that this was a big shot's daughter and could mean big trouble.

But before he could open his mouth, Reshmi began insulting him, in his own language, displaying a repertory of abuses that I found astonishing.

The old man said, But we have a court order! His voice had grown shrill.

To hell with your court order, said Reshmi.

She then barged into the room and proceeded to pick up their belongings, one by one, and throw them out of the window.

Get out! she screamed. All of you! Right now!

Some of the children had begun crying.

What do you people think this is? Some kind of a slum? What kind of people are you, feeding like parasites on the benevolence of someone who is too much of a gentleman to throw you out of the house!

The old man tried to put in words, Look here, lady...

This is not your house, she said, Get out!

We'll call the police, said the old man, and enforce our rights.

Do that, you piece of shit! she shouted back at him. My father knows lots of people in this town. He can bring the establishment down upon you like a ton of bricks. You just wait you son of a three-cornered jam tin!

It took me some time to understand what was happening. Reshmi was talking to them in the only language they understood – the language of power, not the language of rights and obligations.

You-you-you, stammered the old man. You can't throw us out like this!

At this point the woman jumped into the equation.

Who are you to tell us to get out? she said impetuously. We have legal rights and we will stay here as long as we have them. What can you do about it? Go tell your father. We don't care. You big people think the world is your property that you can put inside your pocket. We also have a right to live!

Go live in your own house! Said Reshmi, matching anger for anger. And don't you dare talk to me like that! I'll gouge your eyes out!

You'll gouge my eyes out! said the woman. Just try doing that you hoity-toity piece of flesh.

At this point Reshmi delivered a resounding slap on the cheek of the woman.

Call the police, said Reshmi. Say I slapped you.

The woman instead started screaming at the top of her voice which, in a quiet residential area, could be heard for miles around. The gist of her complaint was that she had not been paid her wages and was being physically assaulted in front of her children.

You can go hang yourself for all I care, said Reshmi. If you don't leave the house immediately, there will be big trouble, I am warning you. You are mistaken if you think that scum like you can just walk into somebody's house and piss all over the place. A bunch of bloody thugs!

She made a spitting sound and then, we left.

Reshmi had not only cowed them down, but also frightened them with her threats of imminent retribution.

And I? I had recovered, as if from an illness, an illness I had been trying hard to disguise as sympathy for the poor, but which actually was a distaste for what they had made out of my life. I was grateful to Reshmi and more dependent on her than ever. She had taken the nonsense out of my life.

I was no sentimental revolutionary. I didn't care for the poor. I was just interested in getting on with my life, my career, get married, start a family, the usual things. Reshmi had given my life back to me.

When we got back to the house in the evening, she went straight up to the guest room door and started banging furiously on it. No one opened. She banged even harder. Open up, you bastards, she shouted, kicking at the door with her high heels. The door remained firmly shut.

They had locked themselves in. I could now sense the fear that lay behind that door, real fear. Fear that I had never been able to arouse in people who, I just realized, were most prone to this emotion. It was they who had succeeded in scaring me.

Was I weak? Or, perhaps too honorable, too scrupulous to even think of assaulting people who were beneath my dignity to attack. Reshmi had no sense of false dignity. She saw things in black and white, like the practical woman she was.

She stood outside the door and abused them in the foulest terms she knew without jeopardizing the social distance that separated her from them. Even with the door closed I could feel the words sinking into them like a chill. A terrifying force of scorned womanhood – had appeared out of nowhere and was frightening them out of their wits.

It made me happy. I was like a child watching his father spank the neighborhood bully.

Reshmi made it a point to do this at least once every day for the time she stayed with me in the flat. She would go up to their room, bang on the door with her fists and then abuse them with the choicest terms. Everyday. It was a ritual that needed to be performed to liberate the flat from their foul presence, to liberate our minds too from the fear they could cause the moment we showed the slightest tolerance for them.

And indeed, Reshmi liberated us both, me from my caustic dread and she, her privacy from their prying gaze which seemed to hover in the air in my flat. We could live again, breathe again.

A few days later, Reshmi's father called to say that the only remedy lay in filing an appeal in the superior court or establishing my claims before the court.

We were back to square one.

When is this fellow in Mombassa going to send in your papers? she asked me, a little impatiently.

They should be here any day now, I said.

Will that satisfy the court? Reshmi asked

Absolutely, I said.

Okay, she said, still a little uncertain about whether I was capable of taking these people on, on my own. I could see she was worried. She had extended her leave by a few days to help me tide over the situation as best as she could, but sooner or later, she would have to get back to her own life.

Are you sure you can handle this? she said.

Yes, I said.

I wasn't sure at all. My spirits sank at the thought that Reshmi was leaving.

Listen, she said. If it gets too much for you, get in touch with these people – she handed me a piece of paper with names and telephone numbers – they are all papa's friends, they will help you find another flat.

Yes, I said, a trifle irritated at her suggestion that I wouldn't know how to tackle these people. If I wasn't equal to this, which she was, then I wasn't her equal.

The letter from Mombassa will be here any day now, I said. I will have the whole thing sorted out in no time and throw these bastards out.

There was a look of helpless agony on her face.

I felt like a worm

On a Saturday evening, Reshini took a flight back to her town. I saw her off at the airport. As she disappeared towards the security, she looked back, smiled and waved. I felt like a prisoner who had just had a visit. She was taking back my inner possessions with her.

As I drove back to my flat, the sky was overcast, and I was going back to a prison, a prison for my inner self, my person. I was going back to a war which would surely resume with redoubled vigour, after all the insult and injury Reshmi had heaped upon them. I braced myself for the challenge that lay ahead, in vain. I was afraid, once again. The memory of my previous defeats lay before me like an obstacle between what I was and what I ought to be, what I should be, in order to be me. This made me furious. I was not easily given to temper. I was aggressive only when defending what I thought to be principles. But I hardly ever chose aggression as a weapon when it came to defending my own interests. I thought that was what society was all about. Values and principles.

I came back to a flat that felt desolate and chilly.

The first sound I heard – a sound I hadn't heard throughout Reshmi's visit – was the ringing of a bell and the blowing of a conch shell.

They had taken no time in detecting that Reshmi had left.

The conch shell was being blown louder than usual. War was being declared.

I went to the fridge, took out a bottle of beer and a can of cocktail sausages, poured the contents of the can onto a plate and then, with all these provisions at hand, went and sat down in front of the television. I turned up the volume as much as I could. Reshmi's influence had rubbed off on me.

Immediately, the door of the guest room opened and the children trooped out in a single file and they came and stood behind. There was no shyness, no hesitation. They had been instructed by their elders.

The talk that followed no longer consisted of guesswork regarding what was happening on the TV. They were passing insulting and derogatory comments on what was being shown, repeating, at the same time, the few English words they had picked up from me, words like 'thank you,' but in mockery. The implication was that I must be crazy or wicked to watch all this.

Some of the comments were aimed at me, although indirectly. When I laughed, for instance, they would laugh after me, a hollow, sarcastic kind of laughter. Mocking sounds, taunting sounds, mimicry, continuously, as long as I sat there.

I turned to them and said, If you don't like this why don't you go away.

Why should we? This was said by one of the boys in the group.

They had been brutally expelled from my world after having gained partial admission. This probably added to their rancor.

Then, shut up, I said, raising my voice a little.

But no sooner had I turned my back than they resumed their verbal onslaught, with their false laughter and gauche mimicry, voices I never thought would resonate in my living room, nibbling away at my intimacy.

The following day was a Sunday.

I went through my usual Sunday motions.

I was coming back from the kitchen, a plate of kebabs in hand, when I was stopped, on my way to the sofa by the little girl with whom I had tried, in my solitude and distress, to establish a tie of affection. She was too young to have grasped the significance or recent events and had assumed that, with Reshmi gone, she could resume her familiar ways with me.

She saw in me her old benefactor, with a bottle of beer and a plate of something to munch on. She looked up at me, smiled and put out her hand.

It was at that point that Reshmi's absence struck me with a sledgehammer force.

Instead of an inestimable woman, full of beauty and intelligence and courage, that I loved, I had this, this little black thing, the tip of her little tongue hanging out, saying something or the other to me, in her tiny voice that conveyed as usual the hectic interaction taking place between her tongue, her palate, her teeth and her sputum, sounds you could hear in the dark, in the countryside, sounds in which delight was taken, as a gift of innocence.

Something came over me. I put the bottle of beer and sausages down on the table and turned around to face the creature who stood in front of me and let out the loudest sound I had ever produced in my life.

GO AWAY!

The girl shook all over, as if struck by a tremor, her eyes grew wide with terror, a rapid stream of urine made a puddle on the floor.

I enjoyed watching that. I felt no remorse. These people had taken away my happiness, my peace, everything I needed in order to believe that I was living my own life and not somebody else's.

The entire gang came out to the living room. They gathered around the little girl who had not yet finished the intake of breath that precedes a bawl and made commiserating sounds, all the while looking at me. There was hostility, of course. But beyond that I thought

I saw other reflexes at work, more mechanical, strategic in intent, seeing how best they could use this incident to fortify themselves and weaken me, morally.

What kind of a jungle man are you? the woman said to me. How dare you shout at my little girl like that? Did she do something wrong?

Why are you people in my house? I said, no longer certain that that was a valid reason for shouting at somebody. It was a trial of physical and moral strength, not of legitimacy.

One of the boys hurled an expletive at me.

I took a menacing step forward.

The mother quickly put herself between me and her boy and said, You raise so much as a finger and I will call the police.

So anguishing was the contrast Reshmi had succeeded in establishing during her brief visit, that everything about them seemed abhorrent to me now. It was as if I was looking at them for the first time. Up until now, my mind had seen them as a part of the indistinct mass of humanity that lay beyond the door to my flat, out of my field of vision, most of the day, who represented for me no more than abstract misery.

But now, I saw them. They were here. Right in front of me. In my living room. Making claims on me. On my biscuits. On my attention. On my affection, even. As if they could have any claim on me beyond the ones that involved the exchange of cash for services rendered or beyond charity.

They had faces that bore the ugly imprint of poverty. Hard faces. I hadn't noticed up until now how hard their faces were. The hardness was not in their features. One could not locate it in a jaw, or a chin or a nose. It was the hardness of life itself. The eyes, black, anxious and watchful, eyes that were like radars scanning the horizon for ever present dangers, but which also had a special opacity that hid their gnawing fear. I did not want to see such faces ever again in my life. I wanted my old oblivion back.

I had already crossed one psychological barrier by shouting at the girl. I was now prepared to cross more. Civilisation, with its sworn affidavits, could wait. This was jungle warfare.

I don't want to see any of you in my living room again, I shouted at them, almost out of my mind, gathering as much force as I could, in my lungs, as much torment in my spirit.

This is my living room, you understand? I went on. Mine! Mine!

They were not intimidated.

So, your wife has taught you to shout at us, has she?! the woman said to me, mocking me.

I lost my mind completely.

I took a step forward and pushed the woman.

She lost her balance and fell on the floor.

The children started shouting at the top of their voices.

The old man cam rushing out of the guest room.

He made anxious inquiries and then looked at me, eyes blazing with righteous indignation.

I heard the children giving him suitably exaggerated versions of what had happened. I had hit her. I had punched her in the chest.

You shameless scoundrel! the old man said to me, raising his voice a little.

You shameless scoundrel! the old man said to me. How dare you raise your hand against a woman?

I will do exactly as I please, I shouted back at him, trying to be like Reshmi, but ending up more like a child throwing a tantrum. This is my house!

They were shrewd enough to realize that my inner essence was not equal to the threat I seemed to be holding out, desperately. There had been too many capitulations for them to forget and revise their opinion about me.

I had used aggression, but they saw clearly that my aggression was not backed by the world. It was the violence of the drunkard. I was never very good at violence. I preferred the quiet resolute authority of my father or Reshmi's father, without realizing that it had taken them many years of patient effort and many failures to acquire it.

The old man had, by now, completely recovered. He was back to his simple, direct ways.

You will pay for this, he said, quietly.

I hurled an obscenity at the old man.

It made no difference to him.

The difference between Reshmi and me was this: she attacked them because she knew she was right, I attacked them because there was pain inside of me.

Even the children could see that.

They followed the old man into the room, looking at me as at someone who had lost his senses, someone who had made a mistake, which was reassuring to them, in a way. They saw, in the way vultures see a man drawing nigh upon his death, that I had moved closer to them, in spirit. They had seen blind revenge in my eyes and it was not a sensation alien to them. It was of their world.

At night, I lay in bed, wondering where I had gone wrong. I thought of my childhood and the spacious and pleasant bungalow in which I was brought up, with the well-tended lawns and the servants milling around, fussing. I thought of my parents, pious upright people who had never harmed anyone in their lives. I thought of my school, my college, my friends.

How good life had been to me, rewarding me with success at every step, always keeping me away from harmful habits and things. A good, clean life.

I had seen nothing wrong with my life so far. But

now I was assailed with doubts. There were things I hadn't learned, things I hadn't been taught. I was groping for the right answers, for the right language, the right gestures. But I felt there was something I didn't know. What was it?

Pure evil.

Or so it seemed to me.

Nothing in the destiny I had assumed was mine made such knowledge necessary. I wasn't brought up to expect evil, to confront it. I was brought up to know the rules and play the game. That's all.

Three days after the 'incident' I came back from work in the evening to find the OC of my than a sitting on my sofa in the living room. Two constables stood behind him.

He got up as soon as he saw me and said, I have an arrest warrant for you. For sexually assaulting this woman.

When he saw my face blanche with fear, he took this, straightaway, as a sign of some degree of culpability, whereas the commotion in my spirit was actually caused by the disproportion between what I had done and the scale of the vengeance that was sought to be visited upon me. Once again, I had been caught off guard, by the audacity of the enemy's lie.

There are two independent witnesses, the OC said.

I was handcuffed, taken away in a police van and put

in lock up. I was produced before a magistrate within 24 hours and then released on bail.

A new chapter in my life had begun.

IV

All my responses dried up. I felt like a shanty town resident who had been bulldozed out of his shanty. Blind fate had been unleashed upon me. I was being exposed to their world, to its precarity, to its undercurrent of brutality. The law was on nobody's side; it was an instrument of fate, like everything else.

My reputation was smeared beyond repair. Word got around, both in my neighborhood and at the office and, although no one believed the accusation, the fact that I had allowed myself to get into such a predicament was held, subtly, against me, as a question mark on my worth as a human being, on the one hand, and on my competence, on the other. I couldn't blame them for feeling this way; such things didn't happen to people like me. I was like a curiosity, a specimen of misery that no one in my circle had ever seen before. Nobody ever mentioned this thing in conversation with me and everyone was uniformly kind and helpful, but I carried my destiny like a stigma, like someone whose inner life used a different set of signs and symbols than those used by the majority, which made it possible for people to share their experiences with each other.

I returned to my house, which was no longer a house, but a living hell.

The only response I could think of was resignation. I shifted the TV into my bedroom and sold off the furniture in the hall.

The other side saw clearly that I had retreated not just from part of my living space, but of my engagement with the world, that I had renounced certain claims over it, under pressure. They interpreted this correctly as a defeat and took over the space vacated by me.

They spread their durries and mattresses on the floor, set up a charcoal stove in the middle and put some idols in one corner. They then settled down to their way of life.

That was not all. They knew they had successfully besmirched me, that a certain number of vital links with the outside world had been snapped and that my isolation was greater than ever. I was a man with a sexual assault case against him, involving a woman of inferior status.

Fear gripped at my heart, all the time.

I was still unwilling to concede defeat, take Reshmi's advice and shift to another house. I would assert my rights in a proper, gentlemanly fashion, without entering into degrading quarrels with people who had no moral right to question them and were, therefore, persona non grata.

So I resolved not to address a single word to them in the future, to ignore their existence entirely and let the institutions deal with them, as they should – impersonally, that is, without taking into account such things as their cunning, their poverty, their fortitude in the face of adversity and their ability to confront their social superiors on their own terms.

I confined myself to my room. But I had no peace. The noise in the living room was constant. These people had made friends in the neighborhood and had constituted their own little circle, partly in order to indicate to me that they were not outcasts in everybody's eyes, that there was another way of looking at things, theirs, which was as strong, in social, if not in legal or even philosophical terms. God alone knew what story they had concocted to justify their impossible situation, but the people who visited them seemed to take as much pleasure at my discomfiture as they themselves did.

A new aspect of the situation revealed itself to me. In the beginning, every time I traversed the hall, there would be an expectant hush, a readiness for battle – these people had no sense of guilt. Their poverty absolved them of every crime. But when over a period of time it became clear to them that I was not interested in a quarrel, they took this to mean, according to their own way of interpreting society not as a domain of rights and prohibitions but as a gladiatorial arena where their strength would be tested and they would emerge either victorious or defeated, that I had, effectively, given up my claims on the living room and they could do what they pleased.

What surprised me the most was the degree of viciousness the children displayed towards me. I could think of several reasons for this. One, I had first cultivated their affection and then rejected it, brutally. It was with the children that I had been able to make full use of my authority, and now, when the sense of my weakness had been transmitted to them by their elders and through direct observation, they reacted as children do, with abandon and rage. They employed a range of tactics to make my life miserable. One of them consisted of deliberately crossing my path before I could react to it, in order to make me break my stride and stumble, especially if I happened to be carrying things.

Or, they would make a sudden noise behind me and when I would turn around, I would see them looking the other way, indifferently. They would mock the way I walked, the way I talked, the deliberately disdainful expression I maintained in their presence and, generally, make as much noise as they could near my bedroom door when I watched TV. They understood that I had rejected them, not as children, but as social inferiors. They took their revenge by playing, precisely, upon this distinction of class, which gave them the freedom of ignoring my sense of propriety and impropriety, whereas I had no freedom regarding their norms.

I realized that the strength of a norm did not depend on its intrinsic worth – it might have none – but on the number of people who adhered to it, defended it.

I told myself that I was standing upon my dignity by refusing to react, but, in my heart of hearts, I knew this was just a pretext, nothing more.

I was impotent. This was how it was. I felt a fury I had never known before in my life. My head was full of violence. I wanted to crush them, annihilate them, subject them to the worst kinds of humiliation, have them savagely beaten up. I dreamt at night of being a military dictator and ordering a genocide. For consolation, my mind would turn towards Mombassa and the precious documents that would soon arrive and liberate me from my bondage.

I called up Mombassa one evening to find out what had happened to my papers. I was told that the landlord had died and his property was under dispute between his three sons. The matter would go to court. So, I had no landlord either. The property would go into receivership and I would have to pay rent to the court-appointed trustee. Buy my rights as a tenant are under dispute, I said. Sorry about that, said the voice at the other end, there is nothing we can do about it.

Nobody could do anything.

I decided to move to another flat.

I got in touch with some of the phone numbers

Reshmi had given me and one of them quickly found me a nice apartment in a pleasant locality. I signed an agreement with the landlord, paid him advance rent for six months and kept the receipt carefully in my pocket.

I sent up a silent prayer and breathed a sigh of relief.

The day the packers arrived to pack my stuff, the old man came to me and said, Where do you think you are going?

That is none of your business, I said.

He remained cool and impassive as ever.

Pay up, he said.

Or else? I countered cockily.

Or else we will take the matter to court and put you behind bars, he said.

All right, I said, go to court.

Just then, the phone rang.

It was my new landlord.

He sounded apologetic and hesitant.

Sir, he began, I normally make enquiries about my tenants before letting out my premises..It is a routine matter. In your case I didn't because you were recommended by Mr X, whom I know and respect.

However, I always make it a point, with working people like you, to check with their offices, about their financial status. And…er…one of your colleagues…I don't remember his name…picked up the phone and told me that you were involved in some kind of criminal prosecution. So, I decided to call up and find out what it was all about, just in case, you know…

I began to see the tunnel at the end of the light. I was devastated.

Yes, I said, and explained the whole thing to him.

He heard me out patiently and then said, See, all my tenants have flawless reputations. My properties are located in respectable neighborhoods. I understand your predicament and sympathize with you, but, I am sorry, I really can't rent out my flat to you under the present circumstances. Maybe later, when you have sorted everything out, I will be glad to oblige…

I tried to say something, but he cut me off, I am sorry, I can't help you. Come over to the office tomorrow and I will refund you.

He put the phone down.

I found that my hands were shaking uncontrollably. I felt something wet on my cheek. I realized I was crying, my whole body was convulsed in pain and grief.

I was an outcast, a rejected human being, a not-good-enough, I had fallen.

It was only after some time that I realized that everyone, the packers, the old man, the woman and the children were looking at me.

I composed myself as best as I could and told the packers their services would not be required anymore.

The old man immediately put two and two together.

I would not be moving out. He could now exploit my situation, milk it for all it was worth, and it was worth plenty.

Something the matter? he asked, again with the hint of a smirk playing around his lips.

I don't know what happened next. Something snapped inside me, under the weight of my accumulated frustration and despair.

I let a loud and prolonged scream, a noise that came straight out of the jungle.

V

It is difficult to describe what became of my life from this point onwards.

I continued for some time with my efforts to find another house, but came up, again and again, against the same obstacle. Nobody wanted a tenant with my "reputation".

My worries began telling on my work at the office and on my relations with my colleagues. They found me strange, irritable, difficult to get along with. My sense of isolation kept on increasing. Reshmi said she found me distant and remote on the phone. I dared not tell her anything about my situation.

She might have found out, though, about me, through her father's friends or have come to the conclusion that

I was no longer interested in her. Perhaps, I had found someone else. The truth however was that I no longer felt worthy of her, having made such a mess of my life. My sense of degradation was such that I felt intimidated at the very thought of bringing her into my life.

One day, I received a letter from her breaking off our engagement. She said I was no longer in the relationship, mentally.

I had nowhere to go, no one to turn to.

I was at the mercy of the old man and his entourage, and he understood this, with his native peasant cunning.

What happened over the next six months after the break with Reshmi was that I came to occupy a no man's land.

A ferocious and ruthless attack was launched, not just on my private space, but on my very dignity. They began speaking to me in a familiar way, calling me by my name in a derogatory way. I could no longer lock my two rooms as before. They had broken the locks. I mentioned the court order, but the old man said he couldn't care less. They could read the fatigue on my face. I was outnumbered mentally and physically. They were wearing me down psychologically, by gradually focusing their attacks on everything that separated me from them. I no longer had free use of my television; the children had learnt how to use the remote and watched films and programmes in their own language, paying no further attention to me. Violence, the rabid, endemic violence of the countryside, hung over the house like a thick fog. When I ate pasta, which I had cooked for myself, with a fork, they would laugh at me derisively.

Is he eating worms, said one of them to the others.

When I tried to read, they made it a point to raise an infernal din and I would be forced to put down the book after a while. They began using my things. My fridge overflowed with vegetables and other strange things, my washing machine, which they had learned how to operate, was full of their clothes.

Thus I found the things I called my own, invested with a strangeness, an alien presence which I found repulsive.

The children followed me everywhere, with their cacophony, mouth-breathing and drooling tongues. They noted everything I did and reported it to their elders. They often asked me questions about some of the things I did and then expressed approval or disapproval. They were horrified when I told them about toilet paper. They sat on the floor of my bedroom, ate there, watching television while they ate, reacting animatedly to everything they saw. They spoke to me sweetly whenever they wanted a favor, but would react with anger and mockery when I tried to rebuke them for abusing my domain.

One night I found two of them, the little girl and an older boy, lying in my bed, the very bed on which

Reshmi and I had made love not so long ago.

I no longer had the mental strength to order them off my bed.

I was dealing with the knowledge that numbers represented a will of their own such that an isolated and ostracized individual could not resist. I could order the children off my bed a hundred times, but they would be back again, the hundred and nth time, just to irritate me, which, in their impoverished world, provided a source of entertainment. It was their revenge for the obvious lack of respect I had for them. I was free to enjoy the luxury of disdain and distance if I was willing to put up with the disorderliness which came along with the worth I attributed to them as human beings.

I kept losing my temper all the time, but to no avail. I found the floor of my bedroom littered and my food processor broken in half. When I scolded them, they laughed. Scornful laughter reserved for someone who did not possess that precious commodity, the only thing they seemed to hold in esteem, above love, above happiness, above the rules of society, a thing they did not posses – power.

I was, like them, powerless.

Everything that set me apart from them was pure charade.

I began drinking heavily, more than I had ever done before in my life, just to forget the pain of an existence

I no longer recognized as mine. I would come home dead drunk, which kind of reassured them, since it was behavior familiar to them. In my drunken stupor, I would forget myself and talk to the children in their own language using the terms they used. This encouraged them to treat me with even more familiarity.

So I drank all the time, to keep myself cheap, to forget my own self-abdication, to abandon the physical effort required to keep reality at bay. Soon, because of my great isolation and because I was slipping up at work and knew that the final downfall was not too far away, I found myself actually enjoying the company of these children, much like a tired taxi driver who has spent the day earning his bread, fighting off hunger and the harshness and the cruelty of the world around him.

But I felt repulsion too and then would sit in a corner and sulk. The children would come up to me and sweetly ask me to play cards with them. They did this out of genuine concern for my well-being. But the thought of hobnobbing with these creatures still unsettled my spirit. I would rebuff them brutally. They would laugh, as if to say, this is your world now. They had reordered the world such that they were in the right and I was in the wrong.

My drinking had got out of hand.

I came back, one night, drunk out of my wits, to the place I could no longer call my home. I went straight to my room, took off my shoes and went to bed. My mind was in a haze. The last thing I remembered thinking was that I was falling from dizzy height into a deep abyss, where a female form was waiting for me, arms outstretched.

The next morning I found myself lying naked next to the young woman, who was also naked waist upward, her hair done, staring at me with soulless eyes.

It took me no more than a second, in spite of a terrible hangover, to realize what had happened. My mind kept saying no, over and over again, even as it gauged the full extent of the horror. Suddenly, my body began thrashing about, from one side of the bed to the other. I thought I was going insane. I did not even bother to cover myself.

Get out! I told the woman.

You are my lord and master now! she said, shedding tears.

I was overcome with nausea.

Get out! I roared again.

She threw herself at my feet.

I have given myself to you, she wailed.

I got off the bed and put on my clothes.

I was very drunk last night, I said, shaking all over, and you took advantage of me.

Who will believe you? she said, regaining her composure as suddenly as she had lost it. There are no witnesses.

You play with my children all the time. You have no friends. Everyone in the neighborhood knows that there is a criminal case against you and that you are a notorious drunkard. Where can you go?

Get out, at once, I said.

Think again, she replied quietly. You will regret this.

I left the house and began walking in any old direction. I walked all day, not knowing where I was going, not knowing what I was doing, searching for something I had lost, but could not find anywhere – myself. I stood in front of shop windows and stared at all the things, clothes, gadgets, books, which had suddenly been stripped of their meaning for me. I stood in front of restaurants and looked at the people inside. They looked far away, their happiness utterly foreign and, yet, only a few months ago, Reshmi and I had had lunch in one of them. Now I was watching a movie in which the main protagonists were other people, people I didn't know. I spent some time sleeping on park benches, loitering about, here and there, like a vagrant. I had no thought, no feeling. It was midnight when I returned to the flat.

The young woman was up - with some food she had prepared for me

I don't want any of your food, I said, and went straight to the fridge to find myself some bread and butter. It was full of vegetables.

I went into the bedroom and closed the door behind me. As I closed the door, I could see, out of the corner of my eye, the woman patiently carrying away the utensils to the kitchen with gestures I had learned to interpret as being those of devotion.

I no longer had the will or the concentration to go to office. After a few weeks of absence, I received a dismissal notice and some severance pay.

And then, suddenly, one evening, a voice began talking in my head, in their language:

So, who do you think you are? The king of the world? You despise us and our lot. Well, as you can see, we are not fools. We are as smart, as persistent and as ruthless as you are. What are you now?

A blob of nothingness. Just like us. God made the earth and made some men masters and some men slaves. Do you think it is our fault that we are the way we are? Look at yourself. Where is your pride now? Who can you throw out, from *your* house? You are a pretty stupid man. Your wife was smarter and stronger. You are weak. You are a coward. You are not worthy of your place in society. You are like a child lost in a jungle talking about rights and the rule of law. You think there is justice? Come and see how we live. Might is right. People take from life what they can get. Life doesn't give away any first prizes. You get a consolation prize if you are lucky.

The rest have to make do with being a part of the

audience, watching the actors perform their parts. We are here only to clap. But destiny has strange plans for the most unlikely people. It gives them a chance to be actors, against all odds. We can also act. It's not fair? What is fair? Life is not about fair play.

ABOUT THE CONTRIBUTORS

Aniket Majumdar *(The Shelf Life)* grew up in Kolkata. A polymath in his mind, he practices marketing research for an institution of higher education and occasionally dabbles in the dark art of writing. He lives with his family in Phoenix, USA.

In the course of her writing, **Anjana Basu** *(Pressure Cooker)* has stalked tigers with ghosts and hunted down bag counterfeiters in the bylanes of Shanghai! Apart from *Outlook Traveller*, she has written for *Vogue India* and *Conde Nast Traveller*. So far, apart from the numerous articles, she has 10 novels, a story flashed on BBC and two books of poetry to her credit.

Debjani Sengupta, translator of *Alam's Own House* is the author of *The Partition of Bengal: Fragile Borders and New Identities* and has edited *Mapmaking: Partition Stories*

From Two Bengals. She teaches at the Department of English, Indraprastha College for Women, University of Delhi. Sengupta's translations have been widely published notably in *Essential Tagore* and *The Oxford Anthology of Bengali Literature (Vol 2)*.

Dibyendu Palit (1939-2019), the writer of *Alam's own House*, is a well-known writer of Bengal who has authored poems, novels, and short stories. His first story, *Chandapatan*, was published in 1955 in the Sunday edition of *Anandabazar Patrika*. A Sahitya Academy winner, Palit pursued Comparative Literature at Jadavpur University and wrote prolifically about human struggles and alienation.

Manjira Majumdar *(No Return Address)* has over time learnt to look at history objectively, especially the events that shaped India's independence. Holding a master's in Comparative Literature from Jadavpur University, she practiced literature in a hurry—that is journalism—for three decades or so. Surrounded by books, window plants, and promiscuous cats, she hopes to write more fiction in the future.

Monideepa Sahu *(Pishi's Room)* is a former banker. Tired of managing money for others, she quit and took to writing. Money still eludes her, though she's authored four books and contributed to a couple of dozen anthologies along the way. She leads a nomadic life. Having lived in New Delhi, Bangalore, Mumbai, Hyderabad and Washington DC, she has made peace with countless creeping, crawling and flying creatures who share her home, currently, in Bhubaneswar.

Rimi B Chatterjee *(About Time, Jessica)* is a writer and academic based in Kolkata, currently working on the Antisense Universe, in which her story is set. The main narrative of this world is embodied in a seven-season TV series which she is trying to get produced before the climate emergency catches up with her. She has three published novels, an academic book, as well as too much short fiction to count to her credit.

Saikat Majumdar *(The Firebird)* is an Indian novelist, critic and academic. He is the author of four novels, *Silverfish*, *The Firebird*, *The Scent of God*, and *The Middle Finger*. His novels primarily deal with themes and subjects like religion, memory, sexuality, history and education. He is a Professor of English and Creative Writing at Ashoka University.

Shoma A Chatterji *(The Woman who Wanted to Become a Tree* and *The Watch with no Hands)*, film scholar and short fiction author rues that she has gone through the struggling gullies and alleys of the publishing world for nearly 40 years. She claims that it still remains an uphill task difficult to negotiate at her age even though the publishers treat her almost like a VIP writer and yet, her painful struggle continues.

Soumitro Das *(The Hunter* and *Revolution)* went to Paris in 1985 with the purported intention of doing a thesis on the novels of Samuel Beckett, behind which lay the hidden intention of learning how to be French. He found love and intellectual fulfillment but destiny then sent him back to Calcutta, where he worked as a full-time journalist with *The Telegraph* and *The Statesman*. Later, he launched himself as a freelancer and churned out fiction—a collection of short stories and a novel.

ACKNOWLEDGMENTS

I, along with my family, dedicate this anthology to my father Pronab Majumdar, who wrote satires and short stories under the pseudonym Omkar Gupta. Hailing from the Rajbari district of Faridpur (now in Bangladesh), he came as a refugee to Calcutta, at the age of 18, leaving behind a large estate. Even through the toil and hardship of building a new life, he believed that a wider exposure helps a human being to grow and expand his heart.

A writer one too many in the family is not good. But it also makes one competitive.

First of all, I would like to thank each and every contributor to this anthology, who so graciously gave me their stories.

My mother, Archana Majumdar, my biggest fan.

My ma-in-law, Ratna Sarkar, who is a storehouse of knowledge and information.

My late father-in law, Mihir Kumar Sarkar, who was my biggest ally.

My daughters, Ishanee and Ima, my harshest critics.

My sister, Soma Mukherjee, who writes better than me.

My life-partner, Judhajit, whose silence speaks louder than his words.

There are others in my journey of life, such as my once revered professors of English and World Literature; my numerous friends and recently, Alisha Verma, my sweet editor.

And Renu Kaul Verma, my publisher, to whom this is more than a mere professional thanks.